Gathering at
God's Table

Katharine Jefferts Schori

GATHERING AT GOD'S TABLE

THE MEANING OF MISSION
IN THE FEAST OF FAITH

KATHARINE
JEFFERTS SCHORI

Walking Together, Finding the Way®
SKYLIGHT PATHS®
PUBLISHING
Woodstock, Vermont

Gathering at God's Table:
The Meaning of Mission in the Feast of Faith

2012 Hardcover Edition, First Printing
© 2012 by Katharine Jefferts Schori

Library of Congress Cataloging-in-Publication Data
Jefferts Schori, Katharine.
Gathering at God's table : the meaning of mission in the feast of faith / Katharine Jefferts Schori.
p. cm. — (Walking together, finding the way)
Includes bibliographical references (p.   ).
ISBN 978-1-59473-316-1 (hardcover)
1. Missions—Theory. 2. Mission of the church. 3. Christian life—Anglican authors. 4. Faith. I. Title.
BV2063.J38 2012
241'.4—dc23

                        2012006910

10 9 8 7 6 5 4 3 2 1

Manufactured in the United States of America

Jacket Design: Jenny Buono
Interior Design: Heather Pelham

SkyLight Paths is creating a place where people of different spiritual traditions come together for challenge and inspiration, a place where we can help each other understand the mystery that lies at the heart of our existence.

SkyLight Paths sees both believers and seekers as a community that increasingly transcends traditional boundaries of religion and denomination—people wanting to learn from each other, walking together, finding the way.

SkyLight Paths, "Walking Together, Finding the Way," and colophon are trademarks of LongHill Partners, Inc., registered in the U.S. Patent and Trademark Office.

Walking Together, Finding the Way®
Published by SkyLight Paths Publishing
A Division of LongHill Partners, Inc.
Sunset Farm Offices, Route 4, P.O. Box 237
Woodstock, VT 05091
Tel: (802) 457-4000   Fax: (802) 457-4004
www.skylightpaths.com

For Bob Ladehoff, who first piqued my interest in the
Millennium Development Goals, the year of Jubilee,
and the machinations of the Lambeth Conference.

Contents

PART V

**The Fifth Mark of Mission: To Strive to
Safeguard the Integrity of Creation, and
Sustain and Renew the Life of the Earth**

Acknowledgments

With gratitude to all the staff of the presiding bishop's office who support this work in so many ways that are rarely recognized beyond the confines of the office: for Chuck Robertson, who does so much significant pastoral and strategic work; for Sharon Jones and her tireless work in scheduling and travel arrangements; for Joseph Mathews and Melissa Rau, who keep the e-mails and letters flowing; for Ednice Baerga, who cheerfully keeps all the minutia related to bishop's comings and goings in order; and to Su Hadden, who looks after hospitality and visitors as well as the arcana of an office building. Neva Rae Fox continues to offer gifted and deeply skilled service in public relations for The Episcopal Church and to offer the latest in fascinating literature. I give thanks for the fruitful and creative ministry of Linda Watt, who looked after the larger staff and operations of the Domestic and Foreign Missionary Society for more than four years; and I gratefully welcome her successor, Stacy Sauls, who is already giving abundant evidence of strategic leadership in that role. My colleagues in ministry—baptismal, diaconal, presbyteral, and episcopal—in The Episcopal Church, the Anglican Communion, and other Christian churches of the United States, are a continuing source of creative stimulation and friendship, for which I am deeply thankful. Nancy Fitzgerald has been a great gift as editor through several books, which would not have come to fruition without her ability to see the broad picture and draw a coherent frame from many moving parts.

And finally, to Dick, who entered this adventure with great love and support at a time in life he thought of as retirement. It is a deep joy to have his partnership, good humor, creative insights, and maintenance skills—domestic, mechanical, and relational!—in the midst of this surprising journey.

Introduction

Most English speakers know something about King Arthur. He presided over a round table in Camelot, where he hosted feasts surrounded by brave and noble knights, whose mission was justice and peace. *Le Morte D'Arthur*, the fifteenth-century compilation of stories about Arthur and his legendary court, reports that his tomb bears the inscription, *Hic jacet Arturus, rex quondam, rexque futuris*: Here lies Arthur, the once and future king. It's a resounding echo of King Jesus, who will return in glory.

In this book, I want to explore the once and future mission of the Jesus people. Beginning with King Arthur seems appropriate, since my own Christian tradition, the Episcopal branch of the Anglican Communion, has roots that spring from the same English soil as the Arthurian legend. The Anglican tradition challenges believers to a radical way of understanding the meaning of mission—being sent out to proclaim the Gospel. It's a challenge not just for Anglicans, but for everyone. The meaning of mission is central to our lives as Christians and indeed to all people of faith. What will storytellers in future generations say about the community of believers? *Missa sunt Christiani, ecclesia quondam, ecclesiaque futuris?* That Christians were once sent out to be the Body of Christ—but will they also be the Body of Christ of the future?

Maybe it's odd to begin a book about church mission by invoking King Arthur. But maybe not. We could go down the lanes and byroads of literature and history, unearthing the myriad ways Christians have echoed the great stories of our faith in their own cultures and contexts. That work isn't finished, of course, and it won't be finished this side of the Second Coming. The way in which the great salvation story has been told or re-echoed in different cultures reflects both contemporary understandings of the meaning of a faithful Christian life and the eternal meaning of abundant life.

I'd like to explore some of the missional history of Anglicanism and indeed all of Christianity and see what it looks like to live a faithful Christian life, sent out by Jesus to love God and neighbor as self. We'll look at mission as it rose both from the Church of England and from the church universal. And we'll peer into the future, for a glimpse of how we might grow into an expanding vision of mission playing out in the particular contexts in which Christians live and move and have their being.

But what exactly is mission? It's about far more than people packing up their belongings and going to Africa or Asia to baptize non-Christians. The meaning of mission is much deeper and broader than that. The word comes from the Latin verb *mitto*, to send. It's the work that Jesus modeled himself and then sent his disciples out to do—feeding, healing, and teaching. The word "mass," and the "dismissal" at the end of the service, are derived from the old Latin command at the close of a service of Eucharist or holy communion: *Ite, missa est*. It means something like, "Go, you are sent." Or as a former bishop of New York used to say, "Get up, get out, and get lost." You've been fed—now get out there and lose your life in service to the world. That's what mission is all about, and you don't need a passport to do it.

The most frequently cited gospel mandate about mission is Matthew 28:19–20: "Go therefore and make disciples of all nations, baptizing them in the name of the Father and of the Son and of the

Holy Spirit, and teaching them to obey everything that I have commanded you." Mission is evangelical—it's about spreading the good news and forming followers of Jesus.

But mission has a broader meaning, too, particularly as Jesus sets out in an earlier part of Matthew (25:34–40):

> Then the king will say to those at his right hand, "Come, you that are blessed by my Father, inherit the kingdom prepared for you from the foundation of the world; for I was hungry and you gave me food, I was thirsty and you gave me something to drink, I was a stranger and you welcomed me, I was naked and you gave me clothing, I was sick and you took care of me, I was in prison and you visited me." Then the righteous will answer him, "Lord, when was it that we saw you hungry and gave you food, or thirsty and gave you something to drink? And when was it that we saw you a stranger and welcomed you, or naked and gave you clothing? And when was it that we saw you sick or in prison and visited you?" And the king will answer them, "Truly I tell you, just as you did it to one of the least of these who are members of my family, you did it to me."

Mission also means caring for the vulnerable. It's a meaning that emerged in Jesus's first public teaching, his inaugural address in the synagogue at Nazareth, when he read from the prophet Isaiah. It's Jesus's own mission statement, a summary of what he himself has been sent to do:

> "The Spirit of the Lord is upon me, because he has anointed me to bring good news to the poor. He has sent me to proclaim release to the captives and recovery of sight to the blind, to let the oppressed go free, to proclaim the year of the Lord's favor." And he rolled up

> the scroll, gave it back to the attendant, and sat down.
> The eyes of all in the synagogue were fixed on him.
> Then he began to say to them, "Today this scripture has
> been fulfilled in your hearing."
>
> (LUKE 4:18–21)

Mission is primarily about how Christians are meant to live their lives, and what actions are asked of them in relation to their neighbors. We might say mission is how to love God through loving our neighbors. The Anglican Communion promulgated a framework for thinking about mission some quarter century ago, called the Five Marks of Mission.[1] It's a helpful outline, particularly in its breadth:

To proclaim the good news of the kingdom. Share the ancient dream of God, spoken by the prophets, about what the world is supposed to look like. That involves living in right relationship with God and one another and all creation. In that world no one goes hungry, the sick receive care and healing, no one studies war anymore, and all live together in peace and justice. Jesus shows us the road toward that reign of God, toward *shalom* or *salaam* ("peace" in Hebrew and Arabic).

To teach, baptize, and nurture new believers. This is about forming disciples of Jesus, people who will share the work of building a world of shalom and who will invite others into those right relationships.

To respond to human need with loving service. Anciently called "corporal works of mercy," this mark of mission is our response to suffering in the world around us as we do the kind of feeding and healing work that Jesus did himself.

To seek to transform unjust structures of society. This aspect of mission is prophetic work, advocacy, politics in the way we more often use the word: Jesus's turning over the tables in the Temple (Matthew 21:12), his parables about rendering to Caesar (Mark 12:17) and the widow's mite (Luke 21:1–4), as well as the vineyard parables about employment and a living wage (Matthew 20). To many Christians this can seem like "secular" work, or too dangerous for religious folk. But it is at the root of our Christian mission to build a society of peace and justice.

To strive to safeguard the integrity of creation, and sustain and renew the life of the earth. This is an area of mission long ignored, but it's intrinsic to a world where all have enough to eat and the opportunity to live in peace. The biblical charge to *"be fruitful and multiply, and fill the earth and subdue it; and have dominion over the fish of the sea and over the birds of the air and over every living thing that moves upon the earth"* (Genesis 1:28) has often been misread. That word "dominion" has been grossly misunderstood to mean "take possession of" and "use for your own personal and usually selfish ends." The word is actually related to *domus,* house, and should invite us to think about caring for the earth as a householder—it is husbanding and housekeeping work.

Mission has not always—or even often—been understood in this broader way in previous centuries. Indeed, Christianity has often equated mission with proselytization. The earliest Christian missionary efforts were about spreading the good news of Jesus and were usually accompanied by efforts to relieve hunger and heal sickness. After the Roman emperor Constantine became a Christian in the early fourth century and made it legal for Roman subjects to be Christians, the mission scene began to change. Christianity began to be associated with citizenship, sometimes leading to forced conversions. The monastic movement emerged at least in part as a reaction to state religion. Mission opportunities expanded in monastic communities, with the scribal work of copying biblical manuscripts, monastic houses of hospitality for travelers, and the development of agricultural practices better suited to local conditions. Gregor Mendel's genetic work on pea plants was a late outgrowth of that kind of practical relief and development work—a concrete example of mission in action.

Yet all through this history is a strong theme of conversion of pagans and infidels—and I use those terms advisedly. Non-Christians were often seen as objects for the action of the Church, rather than subjects in and with whom God might already be at work. Indeed, much of the global exploration beginning in the fifteenth century was underlain by religious and royal orders to colonize and appropriate lands that were not occupied by Christians. Non-Christian territories and peoples were fair game, and European powers looked to the Church to oversee the dividing up of territory. The Doctrine of Discovery,[2] affirming the right of Christians to appropriate land belonging to infidels, has undergirded legal principles of property ownership in the United States since a Supreme Court decision in 1823. The related concept of manifest destiny provided motivation for dispossessing native peoples of lands and cultures, if not their very lives.

The enormities of Christian mission are legion. And yet, in God's economy, there have also been abundant blessings. Selfless service, even unto death, of countless missionaries over the centuries has been offered to heal and educate, feed and shelter, deliver slaves and prisoners, and invite fellow human beings into greater relationship with God and neighbor.

THE MEANING OF MISSION — REMEMBERING THE PAST

The Church of England began to engage in foreign mission soon after its explorers established new venues for colonization and settlement. The first official British missionary went to Goa, India, in 1519.[3] By the late seventeenth century well-developed mission plans for India were emerging, naming seminaries, bishops, and theological and linguistic training as priorities, along with the ongoing work of evangelism and church building.

English missionary societies began to spring up as the seventeenth century gave way to the eighteenth, with the Society for Promotion of Christian Knowledge (SPCK) and the Society for the Propagation of the Gospel in Foreign Parts (SPG) established in 1698 and 1701, respectively. The SPCK focused on printing and distributing religious literature, and on basic education for poor children, both boys and girls. It emerged from the bishop of London's sending of Thomas Bray to Maryland to examine the state of the Anglican Church on American shores. Bray sent back a report commenting on its lack of spiritual vitality, and he eventually went to work establishing parish libraries for the edification of clergy and people in American congregations.

The SPG was instrumental in supporting the presence and growth of the Church of England in the American colonies, both by providing clergy stipends and by encouraging missionary efforts with unevangelized peoples, including slaves.

We mustn't neglect the influence of the Wesley brothers on Anglican mission, particularly in the American colonies. John and Charles Wesley, the Anglican priests who founded Methodism, sailed to the colony of Georgia in 1735, at the invitation of Governor Oglethorpe, hoping to missionize the Native Americans. Their encounter with Moravians on the voyage to the colonies was also a significant chapter in the developing strand of evangelical Anglicanism.

The principal Anglican evangelical mission society was founded in 1799 as the Society for Missions in Africa and the East, though it came to be known as the Church Mission Society (CMS). Among its founders were William Wilberforce and others who sought to end the slave trade. This was the first major Anglican mission group to reach indigenous peoples in Asia and in significant reaches of Africa.

The last of the major British mission societies to be formed was the Universities' Mission to Central Africa (UMCA), inspired by David Livingstone's lectures on his return to England from Africa in the 1850s. Founded in 1857 to promote an Anglican presence in central Africa and to work for an end to the slave trade, it was the first English society to use a model based on sending missionary bishops, and the first to train black Africans as priests. The UMCA was based on an Anglo-Catholic perspective and persisted until 1965, when it merged with the SPG to become the United Society for the Propagation of the Gospel.

The Episcopal Church in America, seeing this rising stream of missionary societies in its mother church, made a different response. Rather than encouraging the formation of a number of different societies, in 1820 it changed its name to the Domestic and Foreign Missionary Society, and decreed that all Episcopalians were members. In The Episcopal Church, we don't have missionary societies—we *are* one, and that has made a significant difference in how Episcopalians have gone about mission work.

Jackson Kemper was The Episcopal Church's first missionary bishop, consecrated in 1835 and sent out to the western frontier to work with Native Americans and settlers. The second one went to Shanghai, and the next to the Ottoman Empire. They were followed by bishops sent to Liberia and Japan. Eventually mission work began in places that were or became effective US colonies: the Philippines, Cuba, the Virgin Islands, Puerto Rico; and in places with American commercial or diplomatic interests: Brazil, Mexico, Panama, Guatemala, Paris, Nice, Rome, and other European cities. Many of those are now separate Anglican provinces; most of the remainder are still part of The Episcopal Church.

We have to look back to the English Reformation and the Elizabethan settlement to make some sense of the variety of mission agencies that flourished in the eighteenth and nineteenth centuries. The Church of England as a separate and established religious tradition really dates to the late sixteenth century, following struggles between the remaining Roman Catholic presence and the emerging reformed or protestant church. Elizabeth I insisted that her people would worship together using a common liturgy in English, but the state would not dictate the particulars of anyone's belief. There is room in this church, she said, for a variety of opinions about hot-button theological issues, which in those days were about just how

Jesus is present in the Eucharist. Three broad parties resulted, or solidified, in the decades after the English Reformation began.

Those parties continue to affect and influence Anglicanism to this day, and they have been an important part of the history of mission. The catholic wing, often called Anglo-Catholic or high church, reflects a strong interest in frequent Eucharist and in a corporate worship environment involving all the senses (color, vestments, candles, incense, bodily actions like genuflection and crossing oneself). The evangelical or low-church party puts more emphasis on the primacy of scripture, the saving relationship between an individual and God through faith alone, and the work of individuals in fostering the conversion of others. The third party is often called latitudinarian or broad church and focuses on maintaining an open posture that includes something from both ends of the spectrum, often from a more liberal or progressive stance. That is a shorthand caricature, lived out in different ways in different ages and contexts, but the three emphases remain active and even activist within Anglicanism today. It's significant and appropriate to observe that in the United States, the parties have historically been less rigidly defined than in England, and that today they are more based on theology than on liturgical practice. A high-church evangelical is not a complete oxymoron in The Episcopal Church!

The mission societies that arose from the different parties in Anglicanism, particularly within the Church of England, sent their missionaries and theologies abroad, to the Americas, to Africa, and to Asia. The reach corresponded to colonial and commercial interests of the British Empire, and the Hudson's Bay Company or East India Company often imported chaplains at some point after establishing a commercial station or beachhead. The theological and liturgical stripe of the nascent Anglican presence often grew within a new colony in a way that excluded the other Anglican parties or emphases. To this day, the style of Anglicanism in the different autonomous parts of the Anglican Communion can often be distinguished and directly related to the mission agency that first sent missionaries.

The churches of Nigeria, Uganda, and Kenya, for example—and indeed much of East Africa—were founded by Church Mission Society workers, as were the small churches in Patagonia (southern South America), which date their origin to a later partner of the CMS. Those parts of the Communion retain an evangelical identity. The churches of central and southern Africa were largely established by SPG or UMCA workers, in an Anglo-Catholic expression.

Something similar happened in the broader Christian mission work in the United States, when the US government divided up Native American reservations among the different mainline Christian traditions, and invited them to operate residential schools designed to Christianize native populations. Presbyterians, Roman Catholics, Methodists, and Episcopalians were assigned different tribes. Today, much of the Navajo nation is Episcopalian, as are the Gwich'in people of the Arctic, and several tribes of the Sioux nation.

But Anglicanism at its best has always insisted that there is value and truth in each of the strands of its tradition—that we need the fervor of the evangelical wing, and the transcendence of the catholic wing, and the wisdom of the latitudinarian. If we lose any of those we are greatly diminished—even blind, deaf, or mute. The Body of Christ needs the ability to see—and to hear, pray, and act—from different and multiple vantage points.

There is a possible seed of healing and reconciliation buried in the midst of the great flowering of mission efforts in the mid-nineteenth century. An Anglican missiologist, Henry Venn, together with a Congregationalist, Rufus Anderson, set out an understanding of mission that moved away from a narrow focus on conversion toward establishing a local expression of the Body of Christ that could develop and sustain its own life as a mature Christian cell. They pointed out that a local church should be self-governing, self-sustaining, and self-propagating, rather than a body whose life was dependent on another for its direction, life, and growth. Here were the seeds of a postcolonial vision of mission.

An American Episcopal missionary, Roland Allen, who worked in Japan and China in the late nineteenth and early twentieth centuries, developed this missionary theology in ways that linked it directly with Paul of Tarsus's work in some of the earliest Christian communities around the Mediterranean. Allen pointed out that Paul brought the scriptures and sacraments and then got out of the way, staying in touch and offering pastoral guidance by letter or a rare pastoral visit. When the gospel has the opportunity to grow and flourish in a new context, it generally does take on a new character; it doesn't clone the original missionary.

THE MEANING OF MISSION — LOOKING TOWARD THE FUTURE

The party emphasis of many mission efforts, whether national, imperial, or theological, was usually an attempt to re-create a church in the image of the missionary sender's church. Yet Jesus has set us free. For freedom he has set us free and sent us out. If he is willing to take that eternal and ultimate risk, can our own mission engagement be any less willing?

We are living with the outcome of centuries of party politics within the church. No part of the church universal has avoided the fallout of narrowed views, and indeed human beings and human communities are constitutionally incapable of seeing the world or the whole church in other than fairly limited ways. Yet we can cultivate a broader view, one that is more consonant with the Body of Christ to which we all belong. And the whole of God's creation is a body of which we are all a part and from which we cannot be cut off.

The body has many parts, none of them identical, each with disparate and valued gifts, meant to be used for the building up of the whole, and indeed, for the healing of God's entire body. We need one another, we need the diversity in which we have been created, and we need to value and empower the varied parts of this body.

The work before us—this mission of God's—is immense, cosmic, even. The world is hungry, thirsty, homeless, sick, lonely, imprisoned, and enslaved—because some parts are. The creation is groaning in travail because of our abuse of the garden in which we have been set. The body is ailing. Joining God's mission is about seeing and responding to that corporate suffering, and beginning to understand our interconnection with the other parts of the body.

That must include a repudiation of party exclusivity and a valuing of the gifts of other parties, even if we do not wholly identify with them. Believing that God is at work in that diverse *other* is the beginning of that valuing.

There are signs of hope in many parts of the body. The church in China today has grown and developed from the vision of Venn, Anderson, and Allen, and calls itself the Three Self Patriotic Movement—in deference to that desire for self-governance, self-sustainability, and self-propagation. Congregations may exhibit recognizable party flavors, but they are held together in one whole, which trains clergy together and governs itself as a national church.

In much the same way, a corporate and global perspective is the only possible solution to our current environmental morass. The same is true of the violence perpetrated on nations and peoples through war and terrorism. Until we have a view that says everyone should have enough to eat, clean water, health care, housing, education, and decent and dignified employment, we will continue to build walls and wars in our own little narrow part of the increasingly fusty paddock. Indeed, we are creating an increasingly fouled sty, far too polluted for any sensible pig. We have something to learn from our non-human neighbors as well as those who are supposed to have greater wisdom.

While we continue to privilege some over others, particularly those who already have wealth and power, we only make the healing work more difficult. Generations who grow up underfed, ill, uneducated, and unemployed will be less able to contribute to the health of the whole body—and the whole body will suffer for it.

I began with Arthur for another reason—his association with the round table. That is a powerfully resonant echo of the heavenly banquet, God's table to which all who hunger are invited. Arthur's companions went and worked in the cause of justice, at least as it was understood in the English Middle Ages. That's our task as well. Jesus's table is open to all and has no seats of greater privilege. There's a wonderful T-shirt that says, "Jesus loves you, but I'm his favorite." All of those seats at God's banquet table are for the favored ones, and that includes all God's people, and all creation. Those who have sat at the banquet table, even briefly, are sent out to gather others to the seats waiting to be filled. There are seats in that festival hall for all humanity, and room for the other members of creation as well.

The Arthurian legends have come to popular consciousness in this age not so much in their own name as in the stories of *Star Trek* and *Star Wars*, ever seeking new frontiers and a society open to all sorts and conditions of creatures, not only human. The great grail myth is told again in *The Lord of the Rings*, and more recently in J.K. Rowling's epic of Hogwarts and Harry Potter. The eternal struggle between good and evil, selfishness and selflessness, which Christians know in the cosmic salvation drama of Jesus, continues to find echoes in unfolding human history.

The once and future king is remembered for his round table, at which those seated renewed their vows each year on Pentecost, when the church universal remembers its founding in abundant diversity. Will the Christian tradition be able to proclaim that God's table is truly open to all, without privilege or penalty, or will we be only a community of the past? Will we continue to grow in humility toward the future God continues to unfold? Are we willing to be sent out to invite others to the abundant feast?

We can only expect to enjoy that feast if we employ a politic that welcomes all parts of the body. That is our part in God's mission. And it's important to remember that it is God's mission, for which the Body of Christ—the church—exists. We participate in helping to build toward the dream God has planted in our hearts.

PART I

The First Mark of Mission

To Proclaim the Good News of the Kingdom

Fear Not

A ngels are personified messages, reflecting the one who sends them. Meister Eckhardt, a medieval mystic, put it this way: "An angel is simply an idea of God." Sometimes the messages get garbled in transmission—that's apparently what happened to the great dragon that Michael the Archangel slew. The dragon's message file got corrupted somewhere along the way. In the cathedral in Stockholm there's an immense bronze sculpture of St. Michael vanquishing the dragon. It shows the grim struggle with evil, but it also gives a hint of the origin of the dragon as a good creature of God. Michael has his foot on the neck of the dragon, which looks very much like a dog with its tongue lolling out.

But the messages and messengers we more often encounter usually get through faithfully. They may be hard to read and interpret, but angelic messages never resort to the puny—they're not text messages: IM HR W8NG 4 U. Those mysterious angelic messengers have a lot more power and complexity, and they almost always start with a blessing: Fear not.

Scripture is brimming with this message. Fear not—God is with you (Isaiah 41:10). Fear not—I bring you good tidings of great joy (Luke 1:30ff). Fear not—I will help you (Isaiah 35:4; 41:13; Jeremiah 32:40; Daniel 10:19). Do not fear—I have redeemed you and called you by name (Isaiah 43:1). My spirit abides among you, do not fear (Haggai 2:5).

Most often the messages are ones of encouragement and comfort, in that old sense of strength: God is near, God is doing a new thing. We live in a world that is desperate for relief from fear. People in the United States are afraid of losing their jobs and homes. Others are afraid of not being able to feed their children or themselves. Many of our politicians are afraid of being chucked out by their constituents if they don't answer their small-mindedness by prompting fear in others.

The angel, though, personifies the message, "Perfect love casts out fear." Guardian angels ward off fearful things and even fear itself. Yet Jesus challenges the disciples who are celebrating their ability to banish demons and earthly terrors by reminding them of what is even more important. He says, "Rejoice at the near presence of God, that your names are written in heaven" (Luke 10:20). Don't put your energy into driving the fear away, or doing battle with it. Instead, remember that God is with you, and you are already accompanied by the sort of love that will never let fear have the final word.

The Hebrew Scriptures remind us that unexpected visitors may turn out to be heavenly messengers—consider Sarah and Abraham, who got a surprise visit from a trio of angels that turned out to be remarkably productive (Genesis 17). The disciples on the road to Emmaus (Luke 24) had a comforting encounter with such a stranger who turned out to be Jesus himself.

In 2008, I was in Sweden for the celebration of fifty years of women's ordained ministry, and Christina Odenburg, the first female bishop in the Church of Sweden, told me about being sent as a visitor. The church was debating whether to remove the conscience clause that permitted men to refuse to work with women clergy. A generation had passed since the first women had been ordained, and many felt it was time to require that all clergy be willing to work with women. The archbishop sent her to speak with a group of men opposed to women's ordination, to inquire about their response to the proposal. When she walked into the room, each one having apparently heard "fear not," they broke out singing "A Mighty Fortress Is Our God"—the verse that says:

> And though this world, with devils filled, should threaten
>   to undo us,
> We will not fear, for God hath willed His truth to triumph
>   through us:
> The Prince of Darkness grim, we tremble not for him;
> His rage we can endure, for lo, his doom is sure,
> One little word shall fell him.

They removed the conscience clause.

What message fells that misguided or corrupted one? Where do you look for that message? Where do you personify it yourself?

The fear all around us cries out for succor and comfort, and if we bear the image of God, we are also meant to be messengers of the holy one—fear not, God is with you. Your name is written in heaven.

The messengers are all around us, if we're willing and able to notice them. Sometimes they come in fearsome guise, which is probably why the ones we recognize as angels have to keep saying, "Don't be afraid," but even our fearful responses can be a reminder to go look more closely. Where would we be if Mary had run away screaming when Gabriel arrived with his message?

The reactivity in our current political situation is filled with messages of fear. Are we willing to receive and listen to the messengers long enough to discover the plea for connection, strength, and loving reassurance? In the midst of the loud complaints about the other party, or immigrants, or people who have a different opinion, there is often a quiet and unheard plea for a community where a person can feel at home and safe. The anger we hear around us is connected to the journey we're on—a search for home, for the dream we share of a world where no one is hungry, or in danger from disease or violence, where neighbors can rejoice together. The mission we share is about that journey toward the reign of God.

Fear not—or at least let go of a little of that fear, and look a little deeper. What's lurking under that dragon flesh? What do you see—anger or angel? It may be a pit bull, or it may be a Labrador retriever, but neither will be tamed by fleeing. Nothing is beyond the reach of the one who came among us in fragile human flesh, who suffered and died as one of us, who pronounced love and forgiveness on those who tortured and executed him.

Fear not, for nothing can separate us from that kind of love. Our names are written in heaven, and so are the names of those for whom we have the greatest fear. Mission fearlessly proclaims that good news.

Making Your Mark

What are you most afraid of right now? A loved one's illness, your job or lack of one, or what the country or your parish church is going to look like next year or ten years from now?

Proclaiming the Good News Relentlessly

Preach the gospel at all times, and when necessary, use words, Francis of Assisi is reputed to have said. Sometimes, Francis knew, words fall short, and our actions are the best proclamation of all.

Not long ago, I spent a day at Christ Church, Fairmont, West Virginia. It's a bustling place, and the hospitality was pretty amazing. A group had been organized to serve lunch to the sixty or so diocesan clergy who were gathered there, and while we were at Eucharist, the parish hall was transformed into a banquet hall, with white tablecloths, each table set with autumn flowers and elegant china and silver. Our meals were served to each of us as we sat at tables, while other workers bustled about in the kitchen, producing the food, serving the plates, and washing the dishes afterward.

During the meal, brightly colored paper stars were passed out, and we were invited to write notes to their rector, who at twenty-nine was facing cancer surgery. The congregation wanted to host the meeting anyway and offer it as a gift to their rector. During the meal a parishioner stood up and offered lament. Underneath her request for prayers was the keening of the whole parish: Why is this vibrant young woman so terribly sick? Why has our shepherd been taken away? What will become of us?

Questions like those haunt all of us at some time or other. That lament is universal. *Why can't we fix it? Oh—God—why?—help!* Human beings want relief from suffering, and we seem to be hard-wired to keep worrying over "why." But in the midst of their sorrow and uncertainty, the people in this parish kept on keeping on. They proclaimed the Gospel through their loving acts for others.

In the gospels, after Jesus warns his disciples not to cause others to go astray, he directs them to forgive anybody who asks, even if it's seven times a day (Matthew 18:6–21; Luke 17:1–6). They react by asking for greater faith to do those hard things. Jesus, though, makes the startling rejoinder: "If you had faith the size of a mustard seed, you could say to this mulberry tree, 'Be uprooted and planted in the sea,' and it would obey you." Mulberries in sea water, indeed! Jesus follows up with a story about the servant's proper role and expectation. Our mission, rooted in faith and strengthened by God, is to proclaim the gospel by sending ourselves out there to serve others.

The story about the master and the servant (Luke 17:7–10) seems to be a way of saying that doing one's duty doesn't get any unusual reward. But it's also a way of saying that faith comes from living faithfully. That is proclaiming the gospel. Faith is not the result of whiz-bang encounters with the holy—it's much more like the creation of coal, through the long, slow accumulation of dead organisms, slowly covered with rock, and then millennia of pressure. Faith comes through the accumulation of life's challenges, maybe like the pressure of being stuck with work or people you wouldn't have chosen, and still finding—and sharing—something life-giving, some grace and blessing, in the midst of it.

The disciples already have faith, but they haven't recognized it. The people of that little parish in West Virginia may not have realized how much faith they really have, but they showed their visitors the results of their faith—and preached the good news—even in the midst of their grief.

So, how does faith increase? Can you drive into this God-station and say, "Check the faith level and fill up the spirit? And while you're at it, would you please clean all those nasty spots off the windshield?" Or better yet, how do we check the faith-meter ourselves?

Consider an amazing story about the work of St. Luke's Church on Wheeling Island in West Virginia. That island was a playground for the wealthy residents of Wheeling a century ago, and today it's a mix of very poor housing, a casino, many of the social ills that accompany poverty, and a few mansions being restored to their former glory. St. Luke's hosts a meal for all comers on Sundays, and in the summer they feed children who don't have access to the regular meals they receive during the school year. They do it on a shoestring—can you imagine providing three thousand meals for a thousand bucks? Who can feed three people a meal for a dollar? When I asked about the funding for their work, they talked about building relationships—because when people begin to see the sacrificial work going on, they respond with donations of food, materials, and cash, or with their own labor. One fellow turns up every year just before Christmas with a significant check, and he vows to keep coming as long as no one discloses his name. These people live in faith, proclaiming the gospel joyfully and profusely, and they see the results all the time. The mulberry tree Jesus speaks about in Luke's gospel is thriving in that salty place.

Faithful living is mostly about spreading the good news through faithful relationships, built and nurtured over the long haul. Congregations will continue to transform lives in new generations when they pay attention to what's important: hospitality, the nurture of children and adults, and radical welcome to all who come seeking God. Faith is fundamentally about relationship—and staying connected and working at those relationships when the going gets hard.

The disciplines of faith are tools for building and maintaining those relationships. Having and working at a regular prayer and worship life is about showing up and being available, being open to transformation in our relationship with God. Anybody who's been at it for a while has experienced periods of dryness and even prayer that feels empty, yet faithfulness means you keep showing up. That kind of faith has its roots in experiences of God that have come unbidden and unexpected, surprising us in the midst of silence or distraction. We know it's possible, so we keep showing up.

That's what Jesus is trying to say in this parable (Luke 17:7–10). The servants who come in from the field and fix dinner are simply doing it because it's part of their faithful service. Thanks aren't expected or necessary—but gratitude is nice when it comes.

All relationships work in the same way. Faithful marriages are about showing up in spite of anger, annoyance, illness, poverty, or simple boredom—because we have the experience and expectation that more is possible. Church communities are much the same. They are laboratories of faith—and factories of faith. When one of us feels lost, there are others to remind us, through the way they live their lives, of the way home. When one is in pain, others offer comfort, reassurance, and hope. You may not see much change in a person from day to day or even year to year, but after a good long time of faithful living, everybody in that community will have been changed.

In the midst of the gathering at that lamenting congregation in Fairmont, West Virginia, someone asked about how to support relatives who seemed to have gone off the rails, helping them figure out where to find hope in the midst of despair. We talked together about the places where we have had our hope answered, where we've seen God's hand at work. Living out our faith and sharing our experience—that's what keeps us hoping and insisting that God will prevail.

Faith and faithfulness mostly have to do with persistence and endurance, mixed with hope. We keep on keeping on because we know God is still at work, even in the midst of suffering, boredom, or emptiness.

We can let the pressure of daily life crush the life out of us, or we can invite that pressure to change us—into coal, or graphite, or diamond. All of those forms of carbon are exceedingly useful, but for different tasks. Even a tiny bit of faith, formed and proclaimed in that crucible, is enough to do remarkable things, whether it's planting fruit trees in the ocean or walking with a friend through the valley of the shadow of death.

Making Your Mark

Where and how is your faith challenged? What ways of faithful living have brought amazing possibilities to our lives? How have these possibilities allowed you to proclaim the gospel to others?

Seeing the Face of Jesus

—⟋⟍—

O ne November a few years ago, I was in New York with only one night available to run an errand. As I started walking across town I began to encounter police barricades—portable fences that get locked together to keep people on the sidewalk and out of the street. As I went, more and more people began to converge and fill the sidewalks. It must be a parade or demonstration, I thought, as the going got slower and slower and I became hemmed in by a sea of barely moving people. I was trapped—there was no way to turn around or get out of that inexorable, surging crowd. Finally we came to a street crossing where there were several police officers. I plaintively said that I had an errand in a store across the street, and an officer opened the barricade and let me cross. I asked him why there were so many people. "The tree lighting," he replied. It turned out to be the night when the Christmas tree at Rockefeller Center was lit, and I was in the middle of half of New York and a hundred thousand tourists trying for a quick glimpse. What were they so hungry for? Was it the beginning of the Christmas shopping season, or a glimpse of the Christ light?

The sea of humanity on that night is probably what Jesus hoped for when he called for a donkey to ride into Jerusalem. No one knows whether it was a small demonstration or if half the city turned out. Yet somehow some tourists from Greece heard about it, and in the confusion at the end of the parade they decided they wanted a closer look. They walked up to one of the disciples and blurted out, "We want to see Jesus" (John 12:21, my translation). They wanted

12

to get a glimpse of whoever convened this flash mob. Was it mere curiosity, or did they have a sense of something deeply significant?

We never learn whether those Greeks got to see Jesus "up close and personal." We do know that Jesus didn't hang around very long: "After Jesus had said this, he departed and hid from them" (John 12:36). Those Greeks were apparently disappointed that day, and that just might be the point. All sorts of strangers want to see Jesus after they get a whiff of something intriguing going on—and many of them are still looking. They may not walk up to us in the middle of a flash mob and ask to see Jesus, but then again, they just might.

Our task as part of the Body of Christ is to get him out of hiding and proclaim his good news wherever we find ourselves. All of the promises—made by our godparents when we were baptized and renewed time and again during the course of our lives—are about that work of getting the Body of Christ and the love of God out of hiding. Part of our mission work is to help let the light of the world shine on a world that often seems very dark. That's what proclaiming the good news is all about.

I celebrated Palm Sunday—*Domingo de Ramos*—once at a farmworker ministry in North Carolina. I was there as hundreds of people gathered under and around an open-air shelter to remember and reenact the flash mob two thousand years ago in Jerusalem. After the service, the elderly priest who serves there told me about the usual housing conditions encountered by many of the farm workers. He showed me pictures of a laborer stretched out on a concrete floor, preferring that to the filthy mattresses spread on cots that were also evident in the photos. Padre Rojas told of the vineyard owner who insisted that he housed his workers in a veritable palace, and that they certainly didn't need new mattresses. When the ministry workers showed up with a truck full of brand-new mattresses, the owner protested loudly, but finally relented. Many foreigners are getting to see Jesus in those fields in North Carolina. I saw Jesus proclaimed and remembered in those actions and in the midst of the fiesta after the service.

In another congregation I visited, we met with military families—active-duty personnel, spouses, and children of those who are deployed, and retired members of the armed forces. All are eager members of that community of love and hope, a shelter in a world of sudden deployments, frequent moves, and for many, growing financial distress. Among those gathered were two young men in the prime of life, each of whom had obviously had significant facial reconstruction. One still wore the haircut of a marine, and the scars of his cranial surgery were painfully evident. Every person there was looking for Jesus, and finding him in the midst of that community. I think I saw Jesus making himself evident, showing his wounds in the upper room where his disciples were hiding. I saw many reaching out to touch him, and others still looking.

"Will you seek and serve Christ in all persons, loving your neighbor as yourself?"[1] All baptized persons are called to proclaim the love of Jesus in their lives, in the unlikeliest places. When deacons are ordained, they are challenged with a similar question and charged to make Jesus and his redemptive love known. Priests are similarly reminded to minister in ways that make the reconciling love of Jesus known and able to be received. Bishops promise to be merciful and compassionate to all, and defend those who have no helper.

Are we showing the face of Christ to the world in the way we love our neighbors? Are we looking for Christ in everyone we meet, particularly the least likely? That is the work of proclaiming the gospel.

Making Your Mark

What about your own desires? Do you have as urgent a hunger as those Greek tourists that fateful Passover week in Jerusalem? Where have you gone looking for—or discovered—Jesus recently?

From the Upper Room to the Ends of the Earth

—m—

R emember the biblical account of Jesus's ascension? A cloud takes him out of their sight, the story reports, and the disciples stand around staring into heaven (Acts 1:9). That is, until two angels come along to see what's wrong. They remind the eleven remaining disciples that he will return in the same way they saw him leave. They're told to stay in Jerusalem and wait for the gift of the Holy Spirit. That's why they go back to the upper room—it's their safe place, their refuge in a storm of uncertainty.

That upper room is the same place where they had the meal with Jesus, where he broke bread and blessed wine, and told them to keep on doing it to remember him. It's the same place where Jesus washed their feet. It's the same place where Jesus turned up after the Resurrection, and came back a week later to talk to Thomas. That upper room is their hangout, their place by the fire, their kitchen table, their local Starbucks. That's where the little community gets together, in grief or celebration. It's also the birthplace of a council circle—eventually that upper room gave rise to countless thousands of churches and communities of Christians all over the world.

When Jesus leaves the earth, the disciples have to start figuring things out for themselves. They can't go ask Jesus what to do next. This waiting in the upper room is a between-time, while they get organized, recover their courage, and wait for a little help from their friend Jesus, in the shape of the Spirit—that visit we mark every year on the feast of Pentecost. This between-time is like waiting for graduation after you've taken all the final exams, or looking for your first job after you leave school.

There's a very interesting collection of folks in that upper room—the eleven disciples who remain after Judas's departure, Mary the mother of Jesus, some other women, and Jesus's brothers. All the male disciples are named, but the women other than Jesus's mother are not, nor are Jesus's brothers. These people form the nucleus of what will eventually become the church—the whole church, not just the Episcopalians or the Methodists or the Presbyterians. The beginnings of all the varied parts of the Body of Christ are found in that group that are gathered in that one room.

Jesus's prayer about that group hints at the difficulty: "Protect the ones you've given me, that they may be one" (John 17:11–21, my summary). The diversity contained just in those two dozen people in that upper room is both gift and challenge. We learn of that challenge almost immediately, as the gift of the Holy Spirit comes at Pentecost, and all those gathered get the same message, even in their diversity. The Holy Spirit keeps them one.

The ongoing challenge of Jesus's friends is their oneness—how to bless the diverse ways in which we have been created and at the same time keep a common vision about where we are going and how to walk the road together. We clearly don't do it perfectly.

The proto-church, that first generation of friends of Jesus, called themselves *the way*—it took a while before they were labeled as Christians, or "followers of the anointed one." It's also apparent that there were struggles even within Jesus's own family. Early in his ministry, Jesus says that those who do God's will are his relatives, not necessarily the mother and brothers standing outside calling for him. His brother James becomes leader of the church in Jerusalem, and his mother Mary is the subject of some tension over who will care for her. There is tension between brother James and disciple Peter over leadership. The women, particularly Mary Magdalene[1] slowly disappear from the church's consciousness, even though it's clear that their hospitality and leadership were essential to the development of the early Christian communities. The Body of Christ has always struggled to stay one, even in the face of human tendencies to say, "I'm in charge," or "I have the full truth"—with the accompanying implication, "and you don't."

The history of the Episcopal part of the Body of Christ is no exception. Some followers of "the way" came to North America convinced of their duty to share their understanding of good news with those who didn't have it yet. They came with the belief that they had found godless savages, that the spirit was absent from this land, and they proceeded to impart the gospel mixed up with a whole lot of other things that weren't exactly good news—at least cultural imperialism, as well as slavery, expropriation of land, and imported diseases, even up to wholesale slaughter. The reality is that none of us ever has a pure and unadulterated message, even if we act with consciously good intentions. We're all limited in our ability to understand and share the gospel. But we always seem to do a better job when we can keep that body together in its diversity.

Keeping the body one has something to do with blessing the other, discovering what is good and right in another person. It's related to our image of the Trinity—one God in three persons, coequal and consubstantial—of the same dignity and essence. The church remains one body when its members are in right relationship, when we recognize the image of God in others and value others as we value ourselves.

Sometimes the early body of Jesus's followers remembered this. Paul challenged those who thought some part of the body was better than another when he said, "In Christ there is neither Jew nor Greek, slave or free, male and female" (Galatians 3:28, my translation). Sometimes the church has assumed that unity is just an internal problem, that if and when it can achieve oneness in itself, the work is done and everybody can rest.

But that search for purity only destroys, usually sooner than later. It leads to death because God is creative, and always doing something new. To deny that creative force is to put ourselves in hell, trying to escape the presence of God at work. We have plenty of examples of that misguided course, from Jonestown to David Koresh at Waco at the more extreme end, to the insistence that all the churches in a diocese have to think and do things exactly the same way, as happened in the Episcopal family in Fort Worth and San Joaquin. In large part, those who disagreed were forced out. That urge had something to do with residential schools and the insistence that Native peoples learn "white" ways. That same search for purity is motivating a lot of the anti-immigrant rhetoric in our country today.

That search for purity is not the road to oneness. We will be one as Jesus and the Father are one only when we can bless the image of God in those who differ, when we can see difference as God's creative spirit at work, giving birth to new life in our midst, when we can value the particular gifts of this community as an expression of God at work, and see the unique gifts of another community in the same way. We are more likely to find that blessed diversity as we come and go between the world and the apparent safety of our church or faith community—our upper room. What if we did what the Israelites were challenged to do? "Put these words on your doorposts and in your hearts: 'Hear, O Israel, the Lord your God is one. You shall love the Lord your God with all your heart'" (cf. Deuteronomy 6:4–9). In all our comings and goings, we need to remember that only God is fully one. We're still on the road.

The upper room is an important way station on the road to oneness, as a place of prayer and nourishment. But we can't stay there for long. We will be sent out to discover and proclaim God at work in new fields, in the variety of God's ongoing creation. We will find oneness in seeking and loving the image of the one God in every creature, as we come in and go out, for in returning and rest we shall be saved, and we shall become one.

Making Your Mark

Where is your upper room? How does it nourish you for the mission of proclaiming the gospel?

Archaeology of Hope

The "Secrets of the Silk Road" exhibition opened a while back in the Penn Museum in Philadelphia. It was scheduled to show mummies and grave goods from interments in western China. At the last minute, however, the Chinese government withdrew permission to show any of the items in the exhibit, and then relented just a bit to permit the display of photographs and a re-creation of the excavation.[1]

The reasons for the controversy seem to have something to do with the identity of the mummies. Most of the ones that have been excavated were buried two to four millennia ago and have Caucasoid features and light-colored hair. Official Chinese history, though, says that this region has been the home of the Han Chinese forever. The discrepancy gives hope to the Uighur peoples, historical residents of the area, who are beginning to agitate for self-determination. Some of the grave goods even have similarities to Celtic textiles—clearly, travelers from all over the known world took this road into the heart of China.

Archaeology has all sorts of outcomes. Something similar went on with the Hebrew prophet Nehemiah, who lived in the fifth century BCE. In the Hebrew Scripture, he relates the story about being appointed as governor of Judea, and returning to Jerusalem (Nehemiah 1–3). After he takes a tour of the city, he decides to rebuild its wall. That wall eventually becomes a symbol and a means of separating the religiously observant Jewish population from foreign and presumably polluting influences. The Jewish population has returned from exile in Babylon, with some memory of better times. Part of what helped them survive their exile was the hope that they would return and once again worship in their former way in the Temple.

The archaeological work of digging into our memories and speaking them aloud can bring new energy, life, hope—and even an experience of resurrection. We can sift through the layers of accumulated life and experience, searching for fragments that will bring that old history to mind. What we discover has something to do with how we search—whether we admit only our own well-remembered experience, or whether we're willing to deeply listen to our neighbors' yearnings and maybe even discover the deeper dreams of an entire people.

Sometimes the memory is only present in the community's history—for the remembered hope is a thing long past. A Native American man in Oregon, who has been working to return the buffalo hunt to his people, knew that his great-grandfather was among the last of the Cayuse tribe to hunt buffalo, in the late 1800s. Some of the tribes around what is now Yellowstone National Park have treaty rights that permit hunting on former native homelands that are now a national forest. Jim Marsh recognized that restoring this ability to his people would heal a lot of old wounds. He got himself elected to the Oregon Fish and Wildlife Commission, and worked for several years to get those hunting rights expanded and restored to the tribes of eastern Oregon. The participation of the Cayuse and Nez Perce people in a recent hunt brought home at least two buffalo to be shared among their people, and the beginning of some spiritual and cultural healing.[2] It was that dream, buried in the history of a people, which ultimately made such healing possible.

Sometimes the historical deposit is rooted in an ancient dream that hasn't yet been experienced—like the ancient prophetic dream of shalom—a healed world where nobody goes hungry or dies too young or lives in fear. That dream is behind the prayer we pray so often: "Your kingdom come, O Lord, on earth as in heaven."

I hear stories about those dreams all the time. Those dreams are what motivate people to change the world around them into something that gets closer to that dream of healed relationships with God, other human beings, and the rest of creation. When Liberians talk about the civil wars there that killed so many people, they will tell you in general terms about the suffering and the murder and destruction, but more often they tell the story of how the peace finally came about. Even when peace talks got started, they never seemed to get anywhere. The warlords refused to make any concessions in the cause of peace—and over and over again, the talks failed. Finally, a large group of market women went to the site of the next round of peace talks, walked in, and said, "We're tired of this. We can't make a living, we can't feed our children, and we're staying here until you figure this out—and you're not leaving." They surrounded the building, they sat down in the hallways and outside the meeting rooms, and slowly the fighters began to open up.[3] Just telling the stories brings healing, even in the face of appallingly violent acts. That's the genius behind the Truth and Reconciliation Commission that Desmond Tutu started in South Africa. When human beings come face to face and let that story come to light, the power of its evil begins to fail. Forgiveness becomes possible, even if it will be years and years in the accomplishing.

We are a people of story. Our most essential mission skill may be the ability to connect our own stories with the big story of how God continues to walk alongside us—from the garden of Eden to the garden of Gethsemane to the hoped for garden of peace. There is something creative in putting thoughts into speech that reflects God's own creativity—in the beginning, God *said*, "Let there be light" and there was light. The entire first story of creation is about

God speaking, God telling the story of how things are to be. In that understanding, all that is comes out of God's memory, God's dream. When we tell our own stories, we are co-creating, sharing in God's creative work, speaking that dream into reality.

Yet we're also sharing God's image with the person who listens. The listener also participates in the archaeological work. A long time ago, Nelle Morton, the twentieth-century Christian advocate for racial justice and women's spirituality, gave us an image of friendship or companionship as "hearing another into speech."[4] The ability to provide that kind of listening space is also a creative act. Is that not what God does for us in prayer? The listener helps create a sacred space in which another's dream or memory is created anew.

Nehemiah's rebuilding of the wall around Jerusalem can be understood in a variety of ways. The reconstruction brought a sense of safety to a people who had been wretchedly vulnerable. But it also walled them off, to some extent, from those in the larger world around them. That wall also brought pride to its builders and artisans—whether too much or just enough pride, we can't be entirely certain. As we speak the stories of our own faith, and listen to those of others, we need to build walls like the ones in an archaeological excavation, flimsy and replaceable markers that keep the field of investigation safe, so that its treasures can be gently released from their matrix, so they won't be stepped on and destroyed by wandering feet. Our boundary markers of attentive and respectful speaking and listening help to shape a creative space.

Inviting others into speech is about building spaces of safety. And once our excavated stories surface, surprising as they may be, we need to find ways to allow them to enlighten others. The stories we share are creative acts, meant to offer the spirit room to work in the world. That's the opportunity we have—to discover the creative spirit of God at work in our speaking and our listening. The holy stories we proclaim need to become living exhibits that tell the truth of God's loving and creative presence to the world.

Making Your Mark

In what ways have you engaged in the creative art of sharing the hope planted in the gospel of Jesus?

Blessing and Hope

Storytelling has been part of the Christian tradition right from the beginning. Jesus looked back through the stories of generations past, retelling the tales of the Hebrew people and their relationship with God, and weaving his own stories of God's presence in his own place and time. The followers of Jesus kept his stories alive, passing them down to new generations of believers—proclaiming the gospel and writing down the stories that we still tell a couple of thousand years later. Today, we still retell the stories of our faith and the presence of God in our lives, for the generations to come need to know them. Our stories are filled with hope—hope for the possibilities of growth and transformation.

Consider the story of the Hebrew prophet Isaiah. His prophecy is offered to people who felt grievously isolated, alone and abandoned, with invaders and occupiers all around. They were living in mortal fear, with enemies on their doorstep. Our own big enemies may be economic or natural disasters, but the fear is the same: *Who will help, we wonder, and how will we survive?* Isaiah confronts King Ahaz about his despair in the face of those enemies, after he's lapsed back into his faithless funk. Isaiah insists—as Jesus does, as we do each time we let the gospel work in our lives—that hope is coming anyway, whether we ask for it or not. Look here, Isaiah says—by the time this young woman gives birth, and before her child is weaned, your enemies will be gone. And by the way, this child will be named Emmanuel: *God is with you* (Isaiah 7).

How and where do we find signs of hope when we're languishing in the dark? How do we discover and proclaim *God is with us*? Saint Columba, a sixth-century Irish monk, is a great example. He wanted a copy of a very beautiful book in another monastery, so he went there and spent months making a copy. When he tried to take it home with him, however, the abbot who owned the original objected. Struggles over copyrights are not new! The two monasteries went to war over the book, and many people were killed. Columba was supposed to be excommunicated, but they let him go into exile instead. After he woke up from his frenzy of envy over this book, he chose Scotland for his place of exile. He went to work there, transforming his despair into hope, and sought to share the good news of Jesus with as many as had been killed in the battle over his manuscript. In the cold, desolate north of Scotland, he founded the monastery on the Isle of Iona—which is even today nurturing Christian community in both new and ancient ways. Hope, new ventures, islands, and the ability to proclaim the good news of Jesus in new lands and new forms—they are equally ancient and postmodern challenges.

God is continually doing new things, and they often come in unexpected forms and surprising places. When people are most discouraged, caught in the deep darkness of spiritual winter, where does God show up? As a babe born to a young peasant woman in a land under occupation. To a monk finding hope in exile, after grievous violation of his monastic vocation. In countless congregations, even today, believers are proclaiming the gospel of hope, too, breaking down the walls that divide peoples of the earth, building bridges to new lands that are also figuratively islands in significant distress: Honduras, Sudan, and Madagascar. We all need to nourish—and tell—the stories of hope that inspire the building of bridges.

There's a prayer we sometimes use at the start of the Episcopal service of Eucharist that offers a guide for nurturing and sharing the story of that hopeful space within us, helping us move beyond the fear and limited vision that can keep us mired in darkness: "Purify our conscience by your daily visitation, that your son may find a mansion prepared for himself."[1]

We tend to lose hope when our awareness gets too muddied and muddled, when we assume there isn't any better possibility, that we're just stuck with the way things are. That's what put Ahaz in a funk back in 700-something BCE, and sent him off to convince one enemy to get rid of another. Columba, too, got stuck in a narrowed view of the world in the sixth century when he began to see his beautiful book as the greatest prize of his life. He found hope when he began to remember a bigger vision for his life's purpose. Mary seems to have dealt with the surprising news of her impending motherhood more easily than her fiancé Joseph did. But then Joseph began to find hope in the midst of a dream, as the angel's words began to expand his idea of the possible.

Those assumptions that keep us bound in darkness are the fruit of fear. When we stop clutching at those tattered, darkening wraiths, and open our hands, hearts, eyes, and ears to the new thing God is always doing in our midst—and proclaim those new things with our mouths—hope is born. The biggest obstacle to hope is certainty—certainty about what is, and certainty about what's possible and what isn't. Hope is rooted in God's possibility, which is always bigger and stranger than we can imagine.

Consider the miracle of the incarnation and its surprising evidence of God doing things far beyond our imagining. When the night is darkest, God answers the dark with the light of the world, Emmanuel—*God is with us*—to whisper hope into hearts that are desperate for a word, a sign that we are not alone, that we haven't been abandoned to the chaos around us. Discovering those signs and speaking those words gets a bit easier with practice, which is why that prayer reminds us about a daily visitation.

Purifying our consciences is lofty language for paying attention to what we focus on—are we, like Columba, obsessed with some *beautiful thing*, or are we simply giving up, like Ahaz? Are we focused on listening and looking for those whispers and wisps of hope that are emerging all around us, all the time? Are we paying attention? Are we speaking up when we notice them? That's really what a cleaned-up consciousness is about, as one of our eucharistic prayers puts it, the ability to notice "the hand of God at work in the world about us"—to notice, point to, and show others the good and hope-filled reality of God with us.

A eucharistic sensibility—that's church-speak for the ability to give thanks—is one of the deep roots of hope. When we remember, and call to mind, and speak of what we're grateful for, we're nurturing that hopeful space, that expectant womb, where God can pitch a tent with us. That's what happened with Mary—she was able to bless and give thanks for her surprising opportunity. Joseph's evident sorrow about his circumstances was transformed into hope and possibility when he let go of his fear and began to give thanks for an unexpected future.

A simple spiritual practice to spend a few minutes doing before we go to sleep and again on awakening in the morning: Notice God-with-us. Keep watch through the day for more wisps of hope. Before we sleep, pray that our dreams may whisper hope in the ear of our hearts. We will have prepared a mansion for the holy one, a tent for God in human flesh, empowering us to proclaim a gospel of blessing and hope to a world bound in darkness and despair.

Making Your Mark

What are you most grateful for? What unwelcome surprises have become blessings?

Leaving Home

A year after the 2010 earthquake, I started Lent at an Ash Wednesday celebration in Haiti, with hundreds of people gathered in the open-air cathedral—a shelter with a roof but no walls, on the grounds of the historic cathedral destroyed in that earthquake. The nation's only philharmonic orchestra, which began as a music ministry at the cathedral, played during the service as the Episcopalians of Haiti sang with a solemn hope and faithfulness, filled with a somber kind of joy. They knew that God was at work, even though the outward signs were small and slight.

In 2010, as Lent followed on the heels of the earthquake, there was very little music, and the sermons were about already having experienced the somber season of Lent and the need to practice resurrection instead. I'm not so certain that's bad counsel at any time, but a disaster challenges our faith and hope in new ways, and calls for new approaches to old disciplines—even the time-honored traditions of Lent.

It probably felt like disaster when God told Abram to go: "Leave your home, your family, the country in which you have grown up. Leave all that behind, in favor of a new land and a new nation, and I will bless you—so much that your name will bless the world" (Genesis 12:1–20, my summary) Abraham was being asked to live his life on the road without all those old comforts or the taken-for-granted stability of home.

29

Jesus himself lived on the road—the son of man with nowhere to lay his head—and his words to Nicodemus say something quite similar: You have to be born from above if you want to see the kingdom of God (John 3:1–21). The kingdom of God isn't anything like what you know now, even if you've seen some hints. It requires dying to the old, choosing transformation, relinquishing the unquestioned and unconscious supports of home, and approaching life with new eyes and new hope. And it means sharing that story of newness and hope with others.

Our spiritual discipline—as Abraham and Jesus discovered—is to practice leaving home, and letting go of the familiar, in search of the new thing God is already doing. It's about choosing life on the road, rather than a settled world where nothing ever changes, and sharing our experience of transformation with others on the road.

When I was in Haiti I met one of our Episcopal missionaries, a young woman who could speak French and had real-world experience of third-world and developing societies, including a summer in Africa. After arriving in Port-au-Prince, she learned Creole, and she functions amazingly well and comfortably in a very different culture than the one she grew up in. She's made a conscious choice to serve in Haiti because she understands the gift and possibility involved in leaving home.

Nineteenth-century missionaries who went out to the frontiers of the evangelized world often went for life, not really expecting to come home again. Some of them packed all their worldly goods up in a big wooden box that was intended eventually to serve as their coffin. The average length of service for those missionaries was four months—most died pretty quickly, of disease or by violence. Yet missionaries continued to choose to leave home. Proclaiming the gospel is about life on the road—and indeed "the road" or "the way" is what his early followers called being a Christian.

The victims of the 2011 disaster in Japan are being served by others who are willing to leave the shelter and comfort of home in search of a new world of healed and restored relationships, bringing the gospel with them in words and actions. In Japan, the earth has moved yet again, and the sea has leapt up and swept the coastlines. Home has quite literally moved out from under many people in northeastern Japan. The aftermath has challenged the courage and willingness of many to go and bless others. The stories of selfless response are being told in quiet ways and only hinted at in other circumstances. Neighbors have reached out to neighbors who were strangers a moment ago, to help look for the lost or the dead, to serve the hungry and thirsty, to shelter the homeless and the naked. Workers in those nuclear power plants left the shelter of safer spaces to try to cool overheated fuel in Fukushima. Some will know illness or early death as a consequence of their sacrifice. They, too, are answering the spirit's call to be born into a world that sets aside fear, demonstrating the good news of love of neighbor, nation, and the larger world. Like Abraham, their names will be a blessing to many, and the members of their nation will be more numerous than if they had not chosen to leave the safety of home. Leaving home has something to do with leaving preconceptions behind, and cultivating an attitude of welcome to all the differences and strangeness we encounter. We will find blessing there as we experience and share our faith with one another.

Among some faith communities, there's a tendency to think that worship is their only significant work. But the reality is that we come together in worship to be fed and equipped for life on the road—we're not meant to spend our lives coddled in the comfort of cozy pews. At the end of the service we're sent out to meet God on the road—in neighbor, friend, and stranger, in disaster and in rejoicing—to preach the good news we've heard at church through our lives. Some new Christian communities are discovering that feeding and nurturing can happen on the road, that they don't need a permanent home for worship, and they make a conscious decision to live lightly on their journeys, meeting in homes, public spaces, or rented rooms. Others decide that the particular ministries to which they're called need more stable facilities, and a building follows. Whatever the case, the real preaching of the gospel happens only when the congregation is dismissed and sent out into the world.

My husband and I had dinner recently with an eighty-six-year-old fellow whose whole life is a witness to leaving home. For more than fifty years, he's been a passionate mentor of young adults—and right now he's eager to go to Japan to help rebuild the social and community infrastructure, if they'll have him. He is deeply invested in God's new creation, happening all around him.

Eternal and abundant life is available to anyone who wants to leave home. When we're willing to suffer the supposed indignity of rebirth, acknowledging that we don't know it all already, we have the opportunity to encounter God already at work in the world around us. Why did God send Jesus into the world, except to invite us into new life and possibility? The road we travel with Jesus may be perilous, it may involve dying to everything we think is essential, but it is the only avenue to new and more abundant life. Go on out there and get on the road and share the good news of a healed world. Happy trails!

Making Your Mark

Where and how are you answering that call to "go, leave your family, home, and nation?"

Tweeting the Gospel

I heard about a parishioner in West Virginia who kept on complaining about the prayer book we in The Episcopal Church still call new. He was really angry about the 1979 Book of Common Prayer, even decades after it had turned up in his church—so much so that he attached a chain to his 1928 prayer book and fixed the other end of the chain to the rack in his favorite pew. When he died not long ago, the congregation cut the chain and put the book in his coffin.

When the first English Book of Common Prayer was published in 1549 and worship began to be celebrated in English rather than in Latin, some parishioners chased their clergy around with pitchforks. An army was raised in Exeter, England, to expunge this heresy—God, they insisted, should only be worshiped in Latin!

One of the central themes of the English Reformation was an insistence that worship be conducted in a language "understanded of the people."[1] Yet in every age, people get comfortable with the status quo and resist change—even the idea of praying in the language of their birth. Native American communities that were evangelized in the nineteenth century often struggle today over whether it's appropriate to use their native language in worship. Some of these struggles have to do with how people regard their native language—some of us, after all, think that older forms and languages are somehow "holier" and that the familiar language of our youth can't possibly be dignified enough to be addressed to

God. In the Roman Catholic Church today, in some places bishops are again encouraging Latin masses.

The linguist Noam Chomsky was once asked what the difference is between a language and a patois. His response? "An army and a navy." A language, in other words, is defensible—it is stable enough to have a society around it that can maintain its borders relative to other languages. What does that say about Latin? The Bible was first translated into Latin in the fourth century, and eventually came to be known as the Vulgate—the common version—for that is what "vulgar" means.

Saints Cyril and Methodius are remembered for helping a local language gain stability and ecclesiastical dignity. They were brothers, born in the early ninth century in Thessalonica, Greece. Cyril was the younger, a child prodigy who gained the chair of philosophy in Constantinople and was put in charge of the library of Hagia Sophia when he was twenty-four. His older brother Methodius was governor of a Slavic colony in the northeastern part of the Greek peninsula. When the king of Moravia asked the patriarch, Photius, to send some missionaries to work with the southern Slavs, Cyril's former teacher decided the brothers would be perfect.

They went, and invented a script for written Slavonic, which eventually became what we call the Cyrillic alphabet. They dignified the vernacular by writing it down. They gave the common language solidity, permanence, and stability—and they insisted that God could and should be worshiped in a tongue "understood of the people."

They met significant resistance from nearby German-speaking clergy, and they couldn't get the bishops to ordain any Slavonic-speaking priests. (The use of religion for colonial purposes is hardly new!) Eventually they went looking for help elsewhere. Pope Adrian II thought their work had merit, consecrated them both bishops, and had the mass celebrated in Slavonic in Rome.

Cyril died soon afterward, but Methodius went back to Moravia and more resistance.[2]

By the time he returned, the Moravian king had been replaced by a nephew who had been convinced by the German clergy that worship in Slavonic was heretical. They threw Methodius in jail, where he remained for two years until the pope bailed him out. The struggle continued for much of the rest of his life, but he did have significant success. At his funeral, which was celebrated in Greek, Latin, and Slavonic, thousands of mourners gathered to give thanks for one who, like Paul, became "all things to all people that he might lead them all to heaven" (1 Corinthians 9:19).

Proclaiming the gospel in the vernacular brings the same challenge in every age. But if the incarnation means anything, it insists that humanity, in all its messiness and even vulgarity, is capable of holding the holy. That includes human culture, in all its evolving diversity. If we cannot tell the old, old story in ways that can be understood and appropriated today, then the Body of Christ is going to the tomb, without much hope for resurrection. Martin Luther wrote hymns using tunes that were sung in the bars of his day. There's nothing intrinsically wrong with lounge music or rap or folk music as vehicles for communicating the gospel.

Those vehicles include the interpretations we lay on the Bible. I read a fascinating exposition by a retired judge from Florida not long ago, whose thesis is to challenge the interpretation of various problematic parts of scripture. He points to the shifting nuances given to passages that treat relationships between men and their wives in translations since the King James. He notes the unabashed sexism in the worldview of those who did that translation, which sees women primarily as vessels for the use of men, in ways that most of us would find pretty crude. He also points to later translations, and their interpretive attempts to be more politically correct, and how that incorrectness is eventually displaced onto relationships between men.[3] You may not buy his entire argument, but simply seeing the shift in interpretation by translators over several centuries is fascinating and instructive.

So how do we tell the old, old story? That is the question and lament that the writer of the letter to the Ephesians is getting at: "In former generations the mystery of Jesus Christ was not made known" (Ephesians 3:5). But how could it be, when there's a language barrier, when the good news can't be understood? In recent centuries, one of the first things missionaries to other cultures have done is to translate the Bible, and it's still a vigorous effort, in spite of the rapid loss of languages across the planet. Yet still we resist hearing the gospel in the vernacular. The 1662 Book of Common Prayer is still the norm in many provinces of the Anglican Communion. Some congregations and dioceses in The Episcopal Church resist new worship language authorized by its General Convention as too "new-fangled."

Telling the gospel story extends to the media we use. Do you know how most people under forty find a church, once they decide that's what they're looking for? In conversation over the back fence—the electronic, web-based back fence. Could that be what Jesus meant in the long ending of the Gospel of Mark? "These signs will accompany those who believe: by using my name they will cast out demons; they will speak in new tongues ... " (Mark 16:17). New tongues, and new ways of speaking—if not new languages—are most certainly casting out the demons of silence and ignorance.

That bit of Mark's gospel also talks about dealing with snakes and poison: "They will pick up snakes in their hands, and if they drink any deadly thing, it will not hurt them" (Mark 16:18). New media certainly come with their share of snakes and poison: scammers who tell you to send money to your friend who's been robbed while on a trip, or the flaming blog posters who would never have the guts to say such things in person. The heart of the believer can deal with those, with charity, accountability, and healing.

The living Word of God continues to speak to those who will translate it into new vernaculars and proclaim it in new ways.

Making Your Mark

Who's tweeting the gospel in your life, in your parish, in your community? Who's rapping the good news of Jesus? What new form or language will you use to tell the good news of a God who loves us enough to enter the world in human flesh?

One Spirit, Many Gifts

What's your idea of the heavenly banquet? Sushi? Filet mignon? Or maybe Death by Chocolate, French vanilla ice cream, and strawberry shortcake? Perhaps you'd prefer a Las Vegas buffet—all you can eat for $9.95. I don't think any of us could eat the same thing for eternity and still find it appealing. Remember what happened to the Israelites, wandering in the desert? They got tired of manna, and whined for meat. God promised them quail, but only quail. Their dissatisfaction had consequences: God tells them, "You shall eat not only one day, or two days, or five days, or ten days, or twenty days, but for a whole month—until it comes out of your nostrils and becomes loathsome to you—because you have rejected the Lord who is among you, and have wailed before him, saying, 'Why did we ever leave Egypt?'" (Numbers 11:19–20).

The variety of a buffet or a potluck is what makes it so enticing. Yet very few of us are sane about our food choices if we're offered that abundant variety at every meal. College freshmen gain weight because of the nearly unlimited variety that's offered in the dining halls.

Jesus, though, tells his disciples to eat what they're offered, even if it's not their immediate preference (Luke 10:7–8). In other words, don't go next door and ask what they're having for dinner. I can remember childhood friends who would ask what was for dinner before they called their parents for permission to stay—and I don't think it was a commentary on my mother's cooking!

St. Lydia's Dinner Church started out meeting in homes in Manhattan. Now the people gather in a Lutheran church on Sunday evenings to cook and share a sacred meal, tell their stories, and build community together. They don't serve the same menu every week, and even if they did, different cooks, ingredients, and happenstance would mean a different result each time they gathered. The same thing happens when we gather at the holy table in our faith communities—the participants vary week by week, even if the wine and the bread don't. But I recently heard a wonderful tale from the dean of a cathedral about how they change the wine with the season—a more acidic red during Lent, and champagne for Easter!

Variety isn't just the spice of life. It's the nature of creation, according to both theologians and scientists. That variety is an expression of free will—and free will doesn't just apply to human beings. All of creation exhibits a certain level of unpredictability, which is what the science called chaos theory is all about.

Healthy communities of all sorts exhibit diversity. Think about a farm field that's been carved out of a prairie. In its original state, there were probably dozens of kinds of plants within an acre, and many, many different insects, worms, birds, and mammals making their living from that abundance. For a farmer to grow a crop in that space—especially the same crop year after year—it takes major inputs of fertilizer and insecticide, and probably substantial use of herbicides. The original prairie is almost certainly far more productive in terms of the sunlight converted into calories—even if human beings can't digest the grasses and insects directly. Creation is meant for diversity, and communities are healthiest when that diversity is encouraged.

One of the gifts of the Body of Christ is its multiplicity—none of us is the whole body; we need the varied gifts of each to become whole. Not all of us are gifted musicians or dancers, TV anchors or deer hunters, Rotarians, Elks, or Lions. We need schoolteachers, nurses, bankers, farmers, fishers, and priests. None of us can do it all. Each one has a part in God's mission to heal the world.

The task of the Body of Christ is to use the variety of gifts we've been given, to love God and our neighbors—and our neighborhood stretches out to encompass all of creation. Loving our neighbors with the gifts we've been given is an essential part of how we love God. The dream of God—that heavenly banquet—needs the gifts of all members of the body: left little toes and right elbows, as well as frontal lobes and eyes. We will not live that dream until all parts are working together as God intended from the beginning of creation.

That's the feast Isaiah talks about—his vision of the heavenly banquet. He calls for an end to hunger, with rich foods and well-aged wines, along with an end to death, tears, and disgrace. That divine and blessed meal (Isaiah 25:6–8) is ultimately meant for all people and all nations, not just one group or one continent. Last time I checked, that vision was a long way off. Yet there are abundant signs of hope—if we peek in the kitchen, we'll see glimpses of the menu being prepared. Cooking up that feast needs the gifts of all sorts of chefs, bottle washers, hunters and farmers, truck drivers and advertisers.

In Washington, DC, I recently met several very remarkable people. One of them is just thirty, and she and several other equally young women started the FEED foundation. She spent the first couple of years after she graduated from college with the UN World Food Program, working to see that school-age children across the world get fed. She decided that a business model might raise more money than she could get out of governments. Her business sells bags that say "Trick or Treat for UNICEF" on one side and "FEED" on the other. FEED has sold half a million bags so far, and schoolchildren have been fed fifty-five million times.

The second person I met started, with a partner, something called Endeavor. Its focus is supporting entrepreneurs in emerging markets. Linda Rottenberg got the idea when she met a taxi driver with a PhD in engineering who wanted to start a business but couldn't afford to rent a garage. Today he runs one of the biggest businesses in Argentina. In exchange for the support of Endeavor, these emerging-market entrepreneurs are expected to mentor others, to return to others the investment of skill, wisdom, and funds made in them—to share their learnings in their communities and beyond.

The third person I met in Washington was Warren Buffett, who talked about the role of business people in making the world a better place. He ended by saying that he and others like him should be paying higher taxes, sharing in the work of building community. You probably know that he's given most of his billions for that same work.

Each one of us has abundance—gifts, strengths, attitudes, abilities. Those are tools for building the reign of God. The only difficulty is that we tend to see those assets as private property, rather than gifts that we steward for a purpose. A complicating issue is that we still tend to talk about ministry as what people with collars do inside buildings with stained-glass windows. Our baptismal covenant reminds us that we are engaged in ministry in every moment of our lives, if we're conscious about it. Paying the bills, voting in elections, guiding children toward maturity, relating to colleagues in the workplace, playing on a sports team, talking with friends and family at the dinner table, and making decisions about what to eat are all part of living as friends of Jesus. Each act and decision can be a step toward that heavenly banquet. And it needs us all—the short and tall, blonde and dark, conservative and progressive—each one of us shares our faith and preaches the gospel through each action we take, each ingredient we add to the heavenly banquet. Come share the cooking, and enjoy the feast prepared from the beginning of the world.

Making Your Mark

What is your part in preparing the banquet?

The Meaning of
Martyrdom

—~m~—

In the Christian tradition, there are two well-known kinds of martyrs—white martyrs and red ones. Red martyrs are the heroes who
shed blood in the defense of their faith, or challenge the principali-
ties and powers of this world, and end up dying because of their
witness—people like Martin Luther King Jr. and Oscar Romero
(the bishop of El Salvador who spoke out against injustice and was
assassinated in 1980). White martyrs are remarkable witnesses to
the way of Jesus in their daily lives, who also give their lives sacri-
ficially, but more often die in their beds—people like Dorothy Day
or Desmond Tutu (and may he live many more years!).

The Celtic Christians saw white martyrs as those who left home
and family behind to follow Jesus on the road—like Columba, the
founder of the monastery on the Scottish island of Iona, or the monks
who wandered the seas in little leather boats, or the ones who went
to Scandinavia to spread the gospel. There's an old Irish tradition
about *glasmartres* (translated either as green or blue martyrs), who live
radically ascetic lives focused on repentance. The color may have
something to do with the skin tone of one who fasts all the time, or
the sense that the ascetic went out into the green and wild lands, in
the same way that the early monastics in Egypt—the desert mothers
and fathers—took the desert as their home.

The first Japanese martyrs were the red sort, persecuted, tortured,
and executed for being Christians. The known history of evangeliza-
tion in Japan began with Francis Xavier in 1549, the same year the

first English prayer book was published. Francis only stayed three years, but left a Jesuit team in place as well as some two thousand Christians. The Portuguese Jesuit mission continued to gain converts, as well as support from the ruling shogun, up into the 1580s. The next shogun, under pressure from Buddhist clergy, ordered the Jesuits to leave but they weren't all forced out. Things got more difficult when Spanish Franciscans showed up in the early 1590s and began to compete for converts. The rumor went around that the Jesuits were Portugal's beachhead to facilitate its territorial conquest of Japan. The shogun executed the twenty-six Christians we remember every year on February 5 and ordered all the Jesuits out. That shogun soon died, but his successor didn't completely enforce the expulsion order either.

In 1600 a Dutch ship limped into a Japanese port with William Adams, on whose story James Clavell's historical novel *Shogun* is based. He stayed twenty years and explained the difference between Protestant and Roman Catholic Christianity to the shogun, which eventually led to expelling all the Roman Catholics. The persecutions, tortures, and executions finally culminated in 1637, which is the last public trace of Christianity until Japan reopened to the West in the 1850s. Yet when that happened, thousands of underground Christians emerged, having passed down their faith, sharing the good news of the gospel from generation to generation without benefit of clergy or missionaries.

That inherited Christianity might be seen as the result of the quiet witness of ten generations and the memory of those red martyrs. It's an example of another kind of martyrdom—the patient endurance of people of faith, caring quietly for their neighbors, proclaiming the good news of God's love in deed when the explicit word is not possible.

Something similar happened in China during the Cultural Revolution. It was a much shorter period, but the work of missionaries that started in the late 1800s grew and flourished during the intense and violent persecutions under Chairman Mao in the 1960s and 1970s. An Anglican priest, Roland Allen, went to China at the end of the nineteenth century with the sense that he should convey the scriptures and the sacraments, and then get out of the way. He insisted that it was Paul's way of witnessing, and that the good news needs some freedom to take root in new soil and emerge as a vine able to thrive in that new soil.

In many places we live with the painful consequences of a form of witness that was culturally bound—among Native Americans as well as in other parts of the globe. Japan, where Christians represent less than one percent of the population, lives with that struggle to this day. Archbishop Nathaniel Uematsu spoke with me about those challenges recently. People there who have received the witness of earlier Christians in one particular form often assume that that is the only possible or correct way of expressing their faith. The Nippon Sei Ko Kai (Japanese Anglican Church) is much tied to traditional ways of worship—ways that do not easily communicate across the chasm between the church and society. We live with the same challenges in the United States—hymns that don't connect with popular cultural idioms, tendencies in some places to use overly directive ways of governing, or an insistence that Sunday morning worship is the only proper witness of the church.

Every person baptized in an Episcopal service promises to "proclaim by word and example the good news of God in Christ." That's being and making a witness—it's martyrdom. Jesus challenges his witnesses to "deny themselves, take up their cross, and follow me. For those who want to save their life will lose it, and those who lose their life for my sake, and for the sake of the gospel, will save it" (Mark 8:34–35). What kind of life are we supposed to lose, and what self-denial—what cross—are we supposed to pick up?

The answer depends on our context, and there is an urgent claim on all Christians, and in some ways it's the same claim on citizens of the United States and indeed of the whole world. The division that's erupted between right and left, between Anglos and Latinos, between "birthers" and "Obamacare" advocates should be evidence. It's the same cross that the Jesuits and Franciscans faced in Japan in the late sixteenth century—and it led to immense bloodshed. God managed some resurrection even in the face of that needless death, yet how much more fruit might have been borne by other forms of martyrdom rather than just the red kind?

All those divisions and positions are maintained by the subtle siren song of self-congratulation: I'm right, and therefore, you are wrong.

At a recent bishops' meeting in Arizona, some of us went to the border where we had the powerful experience of hearing a panel speak about their varied yet direct involvement in issues of border-crossing. The participants included a sheriff, a border-patrol commander, an emergency room physician, a rancher, a community activist, and a pastor who works on both sides of the border. They all agreed that our immigration system is broken, but it was the pastor who built a bridge across the divisions that nailed every one of us.

He told a story about meeting with a group of teenagers and their parents in preparation for a foray into Mexico. One teen's mother challenged him: "Do you support illegal immigration?" He thought and then turned the question around. "Well, I certainly participate in it. I eat lettuce, and I live in a house that was built in the last twenty years, and I like to buy food that isn't terribly expensive.... Ma'am, do you support illegal immigration?"

Almost all of us participate in the divisions that characterize our society. We may not do it through violent language or shouting demonstrations, but most of us have something of an attitude about the people who use words like birther, or call themselves members of the Tea Party, or insist that people on the other side of an issue simply don't understand (because they don't agree with us).

Martyrdom in this context looks like letting go of our self-righteousness. As long as those divisions continue there will be red martyrs, like those shot in Tucson together with Congresswoman

Gabrielle Giffords, whose fate horrifies us simply because their deaths happened in such an ordinary setting. There may be some white martyrs, who leave the safety and comfort of home to go in search of the other, the ones on the far end of whatever position or stance is confronting us. And there may be some blue martyrs who call us all to prayer and repentance for our hardness of heart. And it will take the quiet, careful, and methodical witness of those who will begin or continue to love the other in small and great ways. In our proclamation of the gospel, we need to ask ourselves: What sort of martyr will we be?

Making Your Mark

What sort of martyrdom are you being invited into?

Looking for Life

The history of the old Episcopal parishes in the United States is fascinating. Consider, for example, Christ Church Durham, on the Potomac River in southern Maryland. Over its 350-year history, it's accumulated a vast parish library—it even documents the story of the rector who was jailed for bigamy in 1698. There were times when the future of that congregation looked very dire, but it has survived war and revolution, living through lean years and lusher ones. History and experiences teach us all something about dry bones, and the new life that God breathes into them.

Christ Church may be long on history, but it's probably always been a little short on numbers—fewer than three thousand people live in the town today. Making a living there is focused on the land and the sea, or people survive on what they earn elsewhere or earned earlier in their lives. Yet there are more people turning up for worship on an average Sunday than there were ten years ago, maybe even half again as many. The surrounding community is changing slowly—there are more African Americans and people of Latino heritage, and the percentage of each is increasing, even as the general population is slowly shrinking, getting older, and becoming less educated and less religious than the rest of the state.[1] As it has for centuries, the community there is changing. How will the bones of Christ Church live in the midst of this change?

Think about the gospel story about Lazarus as a challenge to anyone who thinks things are hopeless. God is forever turning death to life for those who are willing to ask, and hope, and see. Asking, hoping, and looking for new life are decisions about how we're going to follow Jesus. They're disciplines that we can get better at, in the same way that athletes strengthen their muscles—we don't call it practicing our faith for nothing!

In the gospel story, Martha and Mary ask Jesus to do something about healing their brother (John 11:1–45). They send a message when Lazarus gets really sick, but Jesus takes his time getting there. When he finally arrives in Bethany, the sisters meet him with their accusations and lament. "If you'd been here, he wouldn't have died," Mary insists. Martha adds that she knows God will do whatever Jesus asks. That may have been as hopeful as either one of them could be.

What do *we* do when things seem hopeless? Not long ago I was walking down the sidewalk in New York City, running errands, when a young Chinese man towing a suitcase stopped me. He looked very puzzled, and a bit frantic, and asked, "Train? New Haven?" We were just a couple of blocks from Grand Central Station, so I said, "The train station is over there." He clearly didn't speak much English, so I offered to show him. He stopped again and said, "Not highway—train?" I assured him, Yes, the train station was right there in that building, over there, even if it looks like an ordinary office building. He still looked very doubtful, but I took him in, showed him the board listing the departure for New Haven, told him he had forty-five minutes before it left, and took him to the ticket counter to buy his ticket. He never would have found it without asking. When all seems lost, we have to ask, and sometimes go looking in places that don't seem particularly hopeful.

I have a friend whose partner died recently, after a four-year journey with cancer. She's written a little book, with a lovely collection of immensely practical suggestions about how to be most helpful to people who are seriously ill, and supportive to them and their families. It includes short chapters about what to do (make concrete offers of help), and what to say (no platitudes, but words of solidarity and understanding). The writing of it has been a very concrete act of hope for my friend. She has found that her sense of God's presence has been reinforced in the midst of the worst trial of her life. At the same time, her offering will bring hope to other people's experience of death, illness, and despair.[2]

We also have to practice seeing new life around us. It's not so hard in the beautiful countryside in the early flush of spring as the whole of creation is practically shouting at us, *Live! Rejoice!* for life has come again after a cold, hard winter. But winter is a different story. So are times of trouble and pain. How do we carry the experience of new life into the depths of winter, or terminal illness, or being laid off, or declaring bankruptcy? It is possible, as our forebears in the faith knew, and as people around us continue to show us. We find new life mostly by looking for it in unexpected places, by training our eyes and ears and hearts to see glimmers of greenness.

We have a choice about how we're going to meet the next surprise. We can ask for new life, hope for it, and look for it everywhere. In the midst of the aftermath of the tsunami it might be praying for the people of Japan, learning more about what's happening, or talking to people here to find some possible concrete responses. We are changed by knowing about it, and we can choose to be changed in hopeful ways, even if our response is to ready ourselves and our communities to respond to the next hurricane right here. We can help fund disaster response, we can pray, we can begin to understand more deeply the interconnections between ourselves and everyone who's suffered from the moving earth—in Haiti, New Zealand, Japan, and Myanmar. We are all brothers and sisters, offspring of the same creator, and even beginning to realize that is a remarkable experience of new life.

Jesus's response to Lazarus's situation changes when he meets those interconnections in a new way. When he first hears about Lazarus's illness, he makes a pretty intellectual response: Lazarus isn't going to die; this is an opportunity to see God at work. After

Mary offers her lament, and he asks where the tomb is, reality begins to sink in. When he begins to experience the suffering of his friends, compassion follows, and Jesus starts to weep. The onlookers say, "See how he loved him." It is that experience of compassion that brings new life into our midst.

How will people of faith continue to love their communities into new and resurrected life? People have been doing it for years, through the good news spoken right here in front of us, through the lives of people who know something about how to bring hope to those in despair.

Ask, hope, see—and see deeply enough to notice the suffering. Do a little weeping—for compassion can be the best motivator to change there is. New life only comes out of a willingness to let go of our complacency that nothing needs to change, or the conviction that nothing can change. New life comes with a willingness to endure the discomfort of discovery, whether it is the suffering of a neighbor or the new possibility God holds out in front of us. Following Jesus and proclaiming his gospel of hope means being willing to weep—and to keep moving down the road toward new life, even after four days in the grave, even after years of suffering.

Making Your Mark

Where have you seen newness in your life recently? Did you reconnect with an old friend? Hear from your children? Meet a new friend, or learn something new?

Living Abundantly

I recently traveled through the vast fields in the green heart of Holland where I saw large numbers of sheep, ranged along the sides of all the highways, and in pasture after pasture in the countryside. They were far healthier and more robust than the sheep Jesus spoke about in the gospel stories and parables.

Sheep in ancient Palestine didn't have access to those lush green pastures, nor to the good veterinary care they get in modern agricultural operations. As a former goatherd, I can tell you that sheep are not very bright. Goats had a bad reputation in the ancient world because they can get through fences and out of almost any enclosure. Sheep are far more tractable, but they can be just as easily led astray as into healthy pasture.

Those who would lead the sheep astray, says Jesus, are thieves and bandits, and they don't bother to use the gate or door into the enclosure where the sheep sleep at night. The wolves or predators who jump the fence are mischief-makers. They can't get through the door because any decent shepherd would keep watch there all through the hours of darkness, literally lying down to sleep in the entrance to the corral. A wolf would have to walk right over the shepherd.

Jesus calls himself the door of the sheep, and says that whoever turns his way will be healed or saved or preserved from danger (John 10:1–18). That's a pretty familiar image—the Lord is my shepherd, leading me to pastures richer than any ever seen in ancient Palestine, to clean and abundant water, along good roads, guiding me with his walking stick and keeping me safe (Psalm 23).

But Jesus uses another surprising image that's easy to miss in translation. He says, "Whoever enters by me (the gate or door) will be saved or healed, and will come in and go out and find pasture ..." and a bit later, "I came that they may have life, and have it abundantly." The word for pasture means something more like "spreading," like that vast green carpet you can find in the lowlands in the spring. A rich lawn of grass and herbs, something only hinted at in the brief flush of growth in the Palestinian springtime. Jesus's sheep pasture is a vision of rich and nourishing food that doesn't end. It's a vision of the garden of Eden, which the children of Abraham have yearned for since they first arrived in that part of the world and discovered how hard it is to make a living off thin, rocky soil.

Jesus is the gate through which his sheep move out into a world spread with abundance, and he says so directly: "I came that they may have life, and have it abundantly" (John 10:10). His people haven't known abundance, but that's what a vision of right relationship looks like—no one is in want, everyone has enough to eat and even enough for a feast.

The psalmist offers a similar image of what this shepherd provides: "You prepare a table before me in the presence of my enemies" (Psalm 23:5). Another vision of abundance meant for human beings is the radical, overwhelming abundance that will put jealousy and enmity to rest and end the striving that characterizes so much of human existence. In the presence of that kind of abundance, there will be no more war.

That is what faith communities are for. Through them, we know something of the abundant, overwhelming love of God because we've been fed at the table. This table is meant to be a taste of that pasture, an assurance that the world God has created is filled with the same kind of abundance. It happens with each celebration of the Eucharist, and each time we share our gifts with the poor and the hungry. It happens each time we preach the gospel with the words of our mouths and the work of our hands.

When I was at the cathedral in Belgium, after driving through those lush fields of pasture and sheep, I heard about the table the community spread for the needy. It's a four-course meal, meant for all who are hungry—children who come alone, just to eat; people who live on the road, without a permanent home; and anyone in need of rich pasture. The community there provides an antidote to thieves and bandits and to those who see the world as a scarce resource to be hoarded or hidden. That place, that corral, is meant to show people the gate, and the widespread experience of abundance. Those people understand that we are all here to taste the banquet, to hear and live the gospel of the one who calls us friend, even though the world might call us competitor or slave or even enemy. Those are bandits' voices. We know the shepherd's voice.

The early Christians described in Acts knew this abundance as well. They shared what they had, and no one went without. They ate in safety, with "glad and generous hearts." Glad and generous hearts are the fruit of not being anxious or afraid, of knowing there isn't just enough, but plenty. That's what abundance produces (Acts 2:44–47).

Telling good news proclaims the abundance set before us. We are spreading rich and nutritious pasture in Haiti, and at the school in Ramallah, and in flood-ravaged communities in the United States. The remarkable thing about this kind of pasture is that it expands as it's shared. There is always more abundance—like the feast for five thousand made from two small loaves and five little fishes. The miracle of the spreading has something to do with how we see, and how we respond. The pasture out there is meant for all God's children. Jesus said quite clearly that he has other flocks, who haven't yet come into his corral, and that he won't leave them hungry either.

What other flocks are out there in the streets of our cities? Who is hungry? Who needs to find the safety of a home paddock? Those are the sheep Jesus is still looking for.

Those who know the voice of the shepherd, and his abundant pasture, are invited to share and do the work of the shepherd. Jesus's flocks are filled with shepherds who will sit in the gate, and go out and lead others to find water and rich, spreading pasture. It's a gift that comes from having grazed here in this field. Rest here a while, and then go out through the gate and find the rich field, and bring others with you. If they also need a place to rest and heal, bring them here.

"You spread a table before me, and my cup is running over" (Psalm 23:5).[1] Those who dwell in the house of the Lord forever don't stay sitting in church, but do remain in the relationship that says, "Be at peace. I am with you. There is nothing to fear" (Isaiah 41:10, my translation). That is what we take with us as we go out through the door. Surely goodness and mercy shall follow us all the days of our life—and surely the shepherd sends us out into pastures of plenty, meant for all.

Making Your Mark

What do you find when you go out that door at the end of worship? Has your vision and understanding shifted enough that you can see rich and spreading pasture? Does your heart sense abundance rather than scarcity?

Nourished by the Word

When was the last time you went to a wedding supper? I was at a family wedding a while back for one of my husband's great-nieces. I've been going to weddings in his family for over thirty years, and the one constant seems to be a dinner after the ceremony. The weddings themselves, however, have changed substantially over the years. Most of them have been celebrated in an Episcopal church on a Saturday afternoon, though there's been an occasional Methodist or Presbyterian one. This was the first one in a wedding chapel, with a nondenominational minister, on a Sunday evening. The preacher had some unusual ideas about the appropriate message for a wedding homily, and although he did talk about the couple being a witness to Jesus's love for the church, he went on to inform the congregation that anybody who couldn't see that was going to hell. He said it not just once but three times, and it produced only nervous giggles from the bride and some of the couple's young friends. We got through the ceremony—vows, a couple of prayers, I now pronounce you husband and wife, and you may kiss the bride.

And then we all slowly filed out of the chapel into the reception area. There was a leisurely opportunity to wander around, greet old friends and family and meet new people, find something to drink and figure out where you were supposed to sit. It was a lovely early summer evening in a place where people could pass freely between the gardens and the glass-walled reception hall. It began to feel more like a loving community gathered to celebrate.

After all the formal photographs had been taken, we were invited to sit and the bride's father warmly welcomed everyone. A blessing was said, and the meal began. There were toasts and speeches, warm and funny, and an evanescent community of love was formed in that place.

That's an image of what Revelation means about the blessing of being invited to the marriage supper of the Lamb (Revelation 19:6–9). The great thanksgiving feast where Jesus presides isn't going to have nervous brides or angry preachers. It will have a community of love gathered around, feasting in the presence of Love itself.

Everyone gets an invitation to that feast—it's not limited to a select few, or however many will fit in the hall. The word will go out, "Come to the feast, and join the meal."

You are what you eat. We do become what we eat, whether it is the holy eucharistic meal or a steady diet of fatty junk food. A big educational push is going on to get Americans to eat a healthier diet, and this time around it shows a dinner plate, with different size divisions for fruits, vegetables, grains, and protein. Veggies and fruit are supposed to cover half the plate, with more veggies than fruit; and grains are supposed to take up more space than protein on the other half.[1] It's a message about balance—and on all levels, from the balance of the scales, to the chemistry of our blood stream, to the state of our emotions, balance comes from eating that way.

The Christian meal of Holy Eucharist is a table spread with abundance, or at least a symbol of abundance. That's one reason many communities use newly baked and fragrant loaves of bread— it's much easier to recognize abundance in that kind of bread. We come together to give thanks for the overflowing love of God, and the message is not really about moderation and balance. Children often understand this in ways their elders have missed or forgotten. I have a friend who tells of her young neighbor returning from communion and saying in a stage whisper, "Mommy, that's the best Body of Christ I ever had!"

The wedding supper is meant to evoke images of delight, a remembered wandering in the garden at the eve of the day, in company with the ones we love, all enmity and division healed and relationships restored. We're supposed to hear God calling in the evening breeze, "Beloved, where are you? Come and join the feast prepared for you from the beginning of the world."

We do become what we eat, and how we eat has something to do with it. Anger ruins the digestion and sours the meal. Gathering in peace with others to celebrate divine, overflowing love makes it far likelier that the meal will prove nourishing. That's why we say, "Peace be with you" to our neighbors before we come to the table. It was a challenge to many parts of the church when we put that form back in the Episcopal liturgy, replacing the part about "If you are in love and charity with your neighbor" or the grimmer piece in older prayer books that warned people not to eat their own destruction. I recall visiting a church years ago where the preacher said, "The peace of the Lord be with you please sit down." The meal was a little dry that day. Abundant life comes from eating abundance, in the presence of overflowing love. Our words to one another change the way in which the meal is received.

We are reminded that bread alone will not ultimately satisfy, but only the word that comes from the mouth of God. What word? The author of the biblical book of Deuteronomy knows the word of God as creative, especially in the repeated refrain of Genesis, when "God said, 'let there be light,' and there was light." Over the six days of that first creation story, God speaks creation into existence; God's word does creative work. That's a significant part of why John's gospel calls Jesus the Word of God—this incarnate word makes creation new.

At the banquet table of the Eucharist we become what we eat— living bread, creative word, love incarnate, abundant life. Whoever eats at that table has life for eternity. But that word-bread we eat is creative. It doesn't just sit in our stomachs. It's supposed to be digested, in order to keep our blood circulating and our muscles moving. Eat—and then go and put your muscles to work in the world. When Jesus says, "The bread that I will give for the life of the world is my flesh," (John 6:51) he's being quite literal—he offers his physical body for the creative work of life. Eat my flesh, he says, and let the flesh that is created be put to work. Eat this bread for eternity—not just to endure, but eat it so that you may participate in the creative work of eternity, building the reign of God. Eat, become a living, creative word, and go out there and make more of it. Spread the good news, the vision of healing, and help the world around you become abundant life.

And when you have given of yourself, when you have exhausted your ability to help the world find heaven, come back and eat again. This banquet table will be spread when it's needed, able to nourish for more creative work. Like manna, we get what is needed for today.

At the eucharistic table, Jesus invites us to come and eat—dinner's on, so come and rejoice at the company of love that gathers, strengthened and nourished by the word of God.

Making Your Mark

How do you find nourishment in the company of others? How does this feed you for the work of proclaiming the good news of the reign of God?

PART II

The Second Mark of Mission

To Teach, Baptize, and Nurture New Believers

Jesus: Our GPS

I had a very interesting experience on a recent visit. The plane I was originally supposed to take had been canceled before the visit, when the airline changed its schedule. There wasn't going to be a flight in time for the meeting that I was scheduled to attend. So I flew to another nearby city, and a man from the diocese I was going to visit agreed to pick me up.

He met me at this airport, which he wasn't familiar with, and after some fiddling around, finally got his GPS working and found the road that "Mildred" told him to take. We took several turns as directed and eventually were on our way down the interstate. I noticed we were on the southbound side of the highway, and though I knew the place we were going was north, interstates sometimes go in very odd directions around cities. I asked if he had a map so I could see where we were, but the GPS was all he ever used. We kept driving, and after a while we began to get into areas that looked pretty rural, and we were still going south. I finally got out my laptop, fired up Mapquest, and tried to figure out where we were. Sure enough, by then we were a good thirty miles south of the airport, going in the wrong direction. We ended up being an hour late for the meeting.

The apostle Thomas had a similar problem when Jesus began to prepare his disciples for his pending departure. "If we don't know where you're going, how in the world are we going to be able to follow you?" he demands of Jesus (John 14:5). Jesus's response?

"I'll show you—I'm your roadmap. I'll be your godward positioning system." If you're connected to that divine roadmap, Jesus implies, you'll discover the way home to God, finding that it's ultimately truer than a compass pointing to the north magnetic pole, and you'll experience abundant life.

My driver that day put all his faith in his GPS, even when it gave significant indications of being wrong. He didn't let go of the error until he was provided with substantial outside evidence that Mildred was leading us astray.

It may seem like a silly example, but what guides do *we* trust, and how do we decide which ones get our full attention? Where and in whom and in what do we invest our full faith?

We live in a nation that is increasingly convinced that our economic woes are tied to Muslim terrorists or Spanish-speaking immigrants, and that our taxes are too high because our government is taking care of people who should take care of themselves. Most of those tax complaints come down to the work of feeding the hungry, healing the sick, and teaching students. Jesus spent his life doing that very work, and when he challenged the governments of his day about their attitudes toward the poor and the least among us, it got him executed.

The world's roadmap definitions of the right direction in life look like accumulating power over other people, and focusing on self-preservation and accumulating the goodies of this world. The shadow side of those attitudes shows up in disturbing incidents that come to light—like the reports of powerful employers exploiting immigrant housekeepers.[1] The roadmap that we have says that poor, foreign women are especially deserving of our extra care—those widows and sojourners whom Israel is repeatedly reminded to safeguard.

Jesus the roadmap is going to lead us down the byways, and into the slums and barrios, and out back behind the big box stores, to find the widows and orphans rummaging in dumpsters for food. Jesus the GPS is going to send us looking for those who are dying of preventable disease—like malaria in Africa, or AIDS in Honduras, or black lung disease in coal country. Jesus the truth-teller is going to send us out to find the lost, who think that more toys in the driveway will make you truly happy. No, this GPS voice of Jesus is going to tell us we're heading in the wrong direction and help us do the recalculating.

When Jesus says, "The father who dwells in me does his works" (John 14:10), he means the works of healing, feeding, and reconciling that restored community and offering more abundant life to anyone who will turn in his direction and take his road. His road is pretty easy to find, once you discover where to look. It's mostly in the direction of the "other." If we're going down the road called "my way" we've probably missed it—that's the wrong highway. Those who take the Jesus way soon discover that it's the way of healing for all—you and me and the whole of creation, coming back into right relationship with God. Sometimes it's called justice, or peace, or shalom, or even salaam. That just might be why in some traditions you turn toward the holy city when you pray—as a reminder that that's where home is, in that vision or dream of a wholly restored world.

I visited a congregation in Sweden recently, where their whole focus is how to serve those who live around them. The worship space welcomes an Eastern Orthodox congregation as well as the sponsoring Lutheran faith community. They make a special effort to invite in those who have no faith tradition—and in western Europe, as in the United States, that is the largest part of the population. The surrounding community is filled with resettled refugees of all different faith traditions, and none, and all sorts of people wander in to light candles or say a prayer. The other rooms in the church building are used for an after-school program that serves all comers, and to gather other age groups in the community. Muslim and Christian children play and learn together, as do their mothers.

After the consecration of a new bishop recently, I met some of the interfaith guests who had joined us. One was Baha'i, another a

Jew, yet a third Muslim. All were part of an interfaith conversation group whose focus is on the kind of reconciliation that we call "building relationships of understanding and discovery." Each one told me how much his own faith had been deepened in these encounters. The conversation among people of deep faith is always about the journey toward God and loving our neighbors.

So what do we do with those words of Jesus? Jesus says that people can see the works of God through him, and that if they want to find God, they should believe in God because of what they see him doing. He also says that if you can't believe in him, then pay attention to who is doing the works of God. Where do *we* see God at work?

The way that is Jesus is about journeying toward God and the other—it's about truth, and it's about abundant life. That GPS comes with a variety of voices, but they all lead us toward loving God and our neighbors.

Making Your Mark

What does your road look like? What does the Jesus road look like in the life of your community? Who is your companion on the Jesus road? How will you help to nurture others on that road?

Nurturing New
Believers

Every new believer whose faith we nurture will continue a journey like Abraham and Sarah's—going off to meet surprising people, in unknown communities, and encountering unforeseen challenges, simply because that's where you've been called to go. We're all on that kind of journey into the unknown, if we're trying to be faithful. We're like the explorers who went looking for the places on old maps beyond the known world labeled, "There be dragons." Journeying is an ancient image for honing the skills and gifts of leadership, and the faithful in every generation are called to equip new leaders.

Leadership demands that we be agents of change, and take others with us. Leading is always a challenging art of character, yet even more so in times like ours, when each turn in the river shows us a new whirlpool or unexpected beaver dam, or spot where the river has flooded its banks, cutting new channels. The voyage is rarely calm these days. These are times for courageous and intrepid leaders, for those who will try seemingly impossible things, and, like Jesus, wrestle with internal demons and more worldly dragons.

In the Christian tradition, leadership begins at baptism. Every part of the Body of Christ shares that work of exploration, navigation, and encouragement into a new future. Faith formation is meant to provide challenges that will draw out those gifts, developing leaders who will spend most of their time *outside* of church, proclaiming the gospel in the messiness of the world. We need to develop and nurture new Sarahs and Abrahams, Moseses and Miriams,

Magdalenes and Levis for the twenty-first century, sharing the faith in every context of their lives, as both followers of Jesus and leaders of others.

We all learn to do things that seem impossible, or at least way beyond what we think we're capable of doing, by being stretched and challenged—physically, spiritually, emotionally, relationally, and intellectually. I believe that activities we consider secular—like rock climbing, proving math theorems, and wandering in the desert—all have significant things to teach the faithful about forming leaders for a new age.

Consider mathematics. It's another lens for seeing the world. My husband is a retired math professor, who was taught over fifty years ago in a school of mathematicians that encourages inquiry-based learning. Students are invited to prove theorems—hard ones that may take months of work to solve—in the belief that what seems beyond us will provide and provoke the most effective learning opportunity. His own work is a good example—in his first academic position, he solved a problem first posed in the 1920s, by working on it for seven years. It was a major risk for a new assistant professor—seven years with no publication probably would end a research career.

That kind of "transformative experience" challenges people to invest themselves deeply in work they may think is beyond them. It shares a kinship with Jesus's forty days in the wilderness, and with the Israelites' forty years of wandering. Those experiences shape and form people who know how to take risks, who trust in something beyond what they know, and who learn how to invite others into similar endeavors.

The same attitude is involved in learning how to climb unclimbed routes on rock faces, or explore new paradigms, or wander into demon and dragon territory. It also has a great deal to do with the new generations of believers being formed in our faith communities.

What does it take to confront a new challenge, to explore new territory, or in those famous words, "to boldly go where no one has gone before"? Captain James Cook said something very similar long before *Star Trek*—that he would go "farther than any man has been before me, but as far as I think it is possible for a man to go."[1] Cook was profoundly skilled technically—he was an excellent mathematician and navigator—and he combined those skills with personal courage and excellent leadership. He knew when to exceed his orders and how to motivate his crew.

Leaders are those who can envision a new or different future and motivate others to go with them. The word for "leading" originally comes from German roots that mean to go, or travel, or guide. Leaders envision a journey, though not always with a concrete and highly particular vision of what the goal is—they go looking, encouraging others to join them. Yet they usually have an overarching vision of that future place or state. Scientific investigators see a mystery to unravel and gather colleagues to accompany them through the labyrinths of discovery. That's what research teams are all about, whether they're focused on hydrothermal vent organisms, the metagenomics of human gut flora, new energy storage technology, or understanding the layers of a palimpsest.

The Abrahamic faiths share a number of traditional images of that future goal: freedom from slavery; a promised land of peace and justice; the blessings of a remembered name, descendants, and a place to root them; a garden where all are fed and live in peaceful relationship with the rest of creation; shalom or salaam. The challenge is forming new leaders who can figure out how to get there.

Each one of us has the capacity to lead somewhere—in the political or arts community, in technical discovery or business methods, in creative and life-giving responses to our growing environmental challenges. But one of the most critical missions of the church is to form leaders—change agents—who can gather others for the journey into an unexpected future, and expand the possibilities by developing other leaders who will transcend the boundaries between those spheres of endeavor.

The great leaders through the ages have often been explorers who have led people into uncharted territory. Rarely have they been solitary seekers—we don't count them as leaders unless they motivate others. The legendary ones, like Odysseus or King Arthur, are remembered for gathering effective teams of colleagues to navigate new challenges. More recent leaders, like Ernest Shackleton or Desmond Tutu, have set out audacious dreams and motivated groups of people to achieve them.

The work of leaders begins with that dream or vision—like Odysseus's dream of going home. That might be an overarching image for all leaders' dreams—a home where there is no more war or dying young or living in fear. Most great dreams partake of that reality, even if the obvious goal is a fuller understanding of the home in which we find ourselves today. It's intriguing to realize that the stories of homecoming from exile in Babylon don't remember individual leaders other than Cyrus, who opened the door (Isaiah 45:1–7). It took a community of leaders, formed in synagogues. Community is both the birthplace of leadership and its goal.

Shackleton dreamed of making a full transit of the Antarctic continent, and when his ship was frozen in the ice and destroyed, the dream continued to be getting his men home safely. Like a modern Odysseus, he led his people through one unforeseen encounter after another, meeting them with creativity, courage, and an ongoing trust that it was possible. He gathered others to his team with a focus on the contribution their gifts would make to the larger goal. He asked the ship's carpenter to join a long and perilous journey in a small whaleboat, even though the man had been insubordinate and challenging. The carpenter rose to the challenge.

Desmond Tutu's dream is founded in the image of the reign of God, the full dignity of all humanity, and an insistence that all God's children are made to dwell together in peace, with justice. He has been fearless in pursuit of that dream, and he has used his remarkable wit both to outsmart any who would forestall the healing of his nation and of the world, and to make their methods seem absurd or ridiculous. Tutu has an impish and ingenious sense of humor, and he's used it to puncture both arrogant self-importance and the insanity of injustice—yet he treats every single human being with profound respect.

Leaders demonstrate a specific set of character gifts, most of which can be cultivated by exercise—or spiritual discipline—and formation in a particular way of encountering the world. The teaching task of Christians is part of building leaders who can dream big dreams and approach them with consistency, who have deep courage, abundant creativity, and a sense of connectedness, which often shows itself as compassion. Learning to do new and challenging things—whether mathematics, mountaineering, or deciphering Hebrew verbs—are all ways of honing these gifts. Forming new believers and nurturing new leaders requires some basic principles.

Consistency. In nurturing faith in new and growing Christian leaders, it's most helpful to keep the main thing the main thing, and encourage all to pursue their dreams with faithfulness and integrity. When an immediate challenge requires a shift in the proximate goal, the overarching vision remains in the mind of a good leader. A worthy goal is not approached by unworthy means, lest it defeat the purpose of the journey. The use of torture or assassination in the expectation that it will end an ongoing conflict is a fitting and timely example. Nor is the goal of a vibrant economy and healthy populace served by gutting services to the most vulnerable populations in a society— something with which many nations are wrestling.

Courage. The courage needed for leadership grows out of the paradoxical awareness of one's own vulnerability. There can be no courage without objective danger—nor is there any courage in foolhardiness. The most effective leadership does not emerge until one has a sense of how that danger is shared by others. The energy for action grows out of urgency, and effective leaders must learn how to name the urgencies, knowing that a failure of nerve in the face of danger only produces greater hazards. There are some rock walls where the only way out is up; retreat is not an option. Global climate change is an excellent example, for denial won't solve the problem— the only way through is engagement and changing the way we live on this earth and use its resources. We haven't yet found adequate leadership to make significant change. Entrenched interest groups are still blowing smoke, trying to mask the real dangers of a failure to act. Those who insist that there is no danger are demonstrably failing to act in their own best interest, relying on their perception of what are at best very short-term rewards. We hope and pray that emerging leaders will find creative ways to expose the smoke for the vanity it is, and effect some transformation.

Creativity. Creative methods, like Tutu's humor, are both a vision of the Divine at work in ongoing newness, and a way to keep us all appropriately humble. I heard him once challenge a group of students to think about their hungry neighbors by saying, "When Jesus said feed the hungry, he didn't mean stand around and wait for pizzas to fall from heaven!" He names the obvious in unexpected images and invites all present into the desperate reality.

Curiosity is another facet of creativity, a searching after it, and a continual recognition that none of us knows it all, or has all the answers—how boring if we did!

Connection. Knowing that you don't have all the answers brings an appreciation of others, and a growing sense of our interconnections. Good and effective leaders discover that the best interest of the leader (loving oneself) is served by attending to the best interest of the whole community (loving neighbor). If part of the community suffers, the whole is limited in what it can do and where it can go. Vulnerability to that suffering—compassion—means teaching our emerging leaders to have open and curious hearts that will occasionally wound them, but expand their compassion and vision in the process.

Our task is to form leaders who build community through con-sensus and collaboration, calling on the gifts of each part of the community to serve the big dream. The dream and vision require a sense of compassion for those who will find any change difficult—but not an empty sympathy that leaves people exactly where they are. The ability to encourage and elicit hope for the future is essential. When we've encouraged new believers to remember the least and the lost and the left out, the nearby and the far away, we've begun the mission work of gathering the whole body to move into the future.

Each and every one of us by virtue of our baptism is a leader called to nurture new believers. Each of us is meant to take the vision planted within us—even if we're still discovering its details—get up and go on out there, and encourage others to join us on the road. We must practice courage, in many spheres of human life—and encourage others to practice courage, too—for new life lies in confronting the fears of change and the unknown and your own incapacity. We must help all people, especially the young, to learn hard new things and find courage they didn't know they had. We must encourage them to go in company—to build new faith communities—for we need each other, even those we find hard to bear. And we must encourage them to take some pizza bakers with them, for there isn't much falling from heaven these days.

Making Your Mark

Where have you helped mentor or nurture new leaders? How are you developing as a leader?

Learning to Be Light

In the well-known story about Andrew and Simon Peter and the Zebedee brothers, they are all invited to leave their familiar fishing work and start a different kind of fishing (Luke 5:1–11). Those two sets of Galilean brothers take to the road with Jesus, and follow him as he tells about the good news of God's reign, feeds and heals people. That's what Isaiah calls shining light on those who have lived in darkness (Isaiah 9:2). And it's what faith communities do in nurturing new believers.

What has brought healing and light to your faith community? Many parishes at some point decided that fishing nets with instructions only in English weren't terribly effective anymore. So they left those nets behind—or at least some of them—and picked up some new ones, with instructions in Spanish. They noticed that the kinds of fish had changed, and that different methods were required.

Time after time, Jesus asks us to let go of the old tools and pick up new ones along the way. We're supposed to go out there and discover people who need good news and light in the midst of darkness—not just wait here for fish to swim within reach of our nets.

The scriptures are filled with images of water and light—the waters of baptism, the waters of fishing, and the seaside highway that Isaiah insists is going to be glorious (Isaiah 9:1–4). Light drives out the darkness, forces the retreat of gloom for those in anguish, and sends Jesus to Capernaum by the sea, bringing light to the coastlands (Matthew 4:12–23).

Where else do we hear about light and darkness, and waters of various kinds but in the beginning of creation, when God creates light and separates waters (Genesis 1)? All of these images are about new creation—the new thing God is doing in the midst of building a beloved community of those who fish for people, bringing good news and healing.

Baptism is about new creation and being children of light. It's an active, involved, ongoing creation in which we take part. It involves change and movement and travel, both getting out of our own way and encountering the vast diversity of God's creation. Follow Jesus; see the world! Follow Jesus, and truly see where the darkness is, where light and healing are needed. Following Jesus is about new birth and bringing in the light.

Yet none of us can produce light all alone, out of nothing. We can reflect it, and we can transform it, and we can produce light from stored-up energy, but ultimately we depend on another source. Baptism invites us to connect with that source of light, then share it with a world in need of it. Our task is to become collectors of light, and to help others become light collectors, too.

If you were a fisherman, what kinds of net would you need to catch light? Think about plants—they're designed to harvest light and turn it into carbohydrates. That's basically where all our food comes from. We would soon starve without the light of the sun and plants to transform the light. Those light-harvesting plants also give us lumber and paper, and they're the source of the coal and oil and natural gas that let us put the sun's energy to work in other ways: housing, transportation, literature—clothing, too—and the energy to run computers, airplanes, cell phones, and organs. Raw material for guitars and food for dancers. What *did* Jesus mean when he said he was the light of the world? It has something to do with light being the life of the world.

Jesus goes to Capernaum by the sea to bring light into the lives of those who dwell in darkness. He calls those four brothers to follow him, to share in his work of lighting the world. Our baptism means the same thing—time to join the body of light-bringers, giving life to the world. When Jesus says, "Repent, for the kingdom of heaven has come near" (Matthew 4:17), it doesn't mean to be sad or depressed. It's an invitation to turn around and face the light. We're meant to be like sunflowers, facing the sun all day long, continually turning to face it directly so they can take full advantage of the sunlight. During the night they turn some more, so that at the first rays of dawn, they're oriented directly toward the rising sun. We're supposed to do the same, leaning toward the source of life, depending on the holy one at work in our midst, and when the night seems darkest, to keep turning in expectation of the dawn.

We're being invited to become transformers of light, and to invite others to the light, so that the light of Jesus can heal and light up the world. We're called to be like sunflowers—and to tend the garden of new generations of sunflowers.

Making Your Mark

Where are you becoming light to those around you? How might you help others be light?

Teaching and Learning the Presence of God

A bout 2,600 years ago, when the kingdom of Israel was conquered by the Babylonians, many of the Hebrew leaders were captured and sent into exile in Babylon. They lived there for generations, feeling lost, empty, and depressed.

The prophet Ezekiel, writing about this time, uses the imagery of dry bones. He speaks of the Jews' hunger to go home, their search for meaning while they live in exile, and their fear that they will die in a foreign land, cut off from home, family, and anything familiar. Perhaps their greatest grief was their sense of distance from God, whom they had worshiped in the great Temple in Jerusalem.

But those dry bones begin to find life as God breathes over them, and as one bone connects to another. As they remember who they are—and that God cares deeply for them—they begin to find hope.

Is there any parallel with the experience of people from Latin America who have come to the United States seeking a way to survive? The United States has certainly been called Babylon before! The Hebrew people who went to Babylon did not go willingly, but if they had stayed in Jerusalem they would almost certainly have died there. In Babylon, they were hostages, captives, and maybe even something like slaves.

Migration is usually a necessity, not a completely free choice. Many of the people who live in North America now are the descendents of those who have come here seeking life—the Irish fleeing famine, the transported English convicts sent here centuries ago and promised freedom if they would work as servants for several years. Africans were sent here as slaves—and they, too, kept looking for life and meaning in the midst of their suffering. The biblical story of dry bones (Ezekiel 37:1–14). was one of the places they found hope. It offers an answer to the question, "Can we possibly survive in this foreign land?"

When they could no longer worship in the Temple in Jerusalem, the exiles in Babylon looked for new ways to connect with God. Synagogues developed out of that experience of exile, and so did many of the worship practices that characterize Judaism to this day. Theological ideas also developed—final judgment, resurrection, angels—and so did much of the yearning for a deliverer, a messiah, who would set the people free and let them go home again. The Christian season of Advent springs from that same yearning. Jews still wait for the messiah. Christians believe that he has come, that he is among us still, and that he will come again at the end of time.

John of Damascus lived in the eighth century in Syria. A priest and monk, he worked for the caliph, the Muslim ruler in Damascus, as head of the royal treasury. He was also the official ambassador to the caliph for the Christian community in Damascus. He's best remembered for the writing he did in defense of using icons and images in churches.

The Byzantine emperor Leo III had forbidden the use of icons, insisting that they be destroyed and persecuting the monasteries where many were produced. But John defended their use and helped others to see the difference between the worship we offer only to God and the reverence we have for icons and images that help us to see and understand God's presence in the world around us.

Icons and images are important in many Christian communities, and different communities use different ones because they help us understand the presence of God in our own particular context. The Hebrew exiles in Babylon found new forms of worship that helped them find God in their context, and synagogues have continued to be of great importance. The Mass we know in church is a further development from the form of worship used in synagogues. Mexican Christians have brought *posadas*—reenactments of the Nativity—and devotion to Our Lady of Guadalupe as they migrated to the United States. Other Latin American cultures have found God through other visions of Mary, other saints, other songs and customs. The Africans who were brought here as slaves discovered God in new ways through the gospel their masters shared—and the musical form of spirituals provides another rich set of icons. The wider Christian community has always been enriched by discovering God through new images in new contexts.

Icons are road signs for those in exile—and we're all in exile. None of us yet lives in the fullness of God's kingdom. We wait expectantly for God's inbreaking. The images of God all around us—the human beings, as well as the ways we write, sing, paint, and dance about God—are a promise of God's presence among us. All these can be icons of the Divine. They are signs on the road—home is this way, do you see?

Forming new believers includes the invitation to discover God's presence around and within them in ways that may surprise their elders in the faith. The creative light of God continues to shine forth in new ways. Even in darkness, there is always a glimpse of light. Even in exile, there is hope. The varied icons of our communities can deepen faith.

Making Your Mark

In what unexpected ways have you discovered God's presence in your life? Have you ever gathered with others to share some of those stories?

On the Road

I spent a lot of time in the college chapel when I was a teenager. I started college when I was just sixteen, before I could legally drive. One of the women in my dorm borrowed a car and took me to get my driver's license—after I promised to teach her how to drive a stick shift! Being younger than most of my classmates, feeling like a geek, and having a whole lot of questions, brought me into the chapel a lot of times in the middle of the night. I was grateful for the refuge and the solace it offered me then.

I entered college as an Episcopalian and a science major, uncertain whether I wanted eventually to go to medical school or study the amazing creatures that live in the ocean. I also came full of things I wanted to learn, like how to SCUBA dive and how to fly, and like other freshmen, I struggled through calculus and organic chemistry. But what sent me to the chapel in the middle of the night had more to do with big questions about relationship—between human beings, in that challenging reality called love—and about the relationship between being a Christian and a scientist. I'm not sure I found a whole lot of answers at midnight, but I did find some reassurance that I wasn't alone with those questions. I came to know that even when I was the only person in the chapel, I wasn't all alone.

That's the same kind of human longing that Jesus and his disciples wrestled with. As he starts to leave his disciples they're not quite sure they're ready to let him go. It's sort of like parents dropping their kids off at college. Leaving the familiar is both a thrilling and a daunting adventure, and those disciples out in Bethany aren't sure they're ready for the next chapter of the learning adventure called life in Jesus (Luke 24:50–53).

The beginning of Acts (Acts1:9–11) offers a wonderful image of those disciples caught in their trepidation as the next chapter begins: They watch as a cloud takes Jesus out of sight, then they stand around and gaze toward heaven. There are lots of stained glass windows that show Jesus's feet hanging out from under a cloud, and the disciples standing around with their mouths open—you can imagine them perplexed and wondering, "*Now* what? We're supposed to figure this out on our own?" And as I heard one preacher say, Luke's version is far too rosy—your trusted teacher, beloved elder brother, and best friend leaves town and you go back to church and *rejoice?*

Jesus's ascension is a great deal like leaving home and setting out in the world on your own—except that none of us is ever all alone. It takes us a while to figure out, or remember, that Jesus is still here, that our family still wants to hear from us and offer support, that we *are* going to find new friends and community and support in a new chapter of possibility. But it can sure be scary.

Life is a challenge, and most of us are afraid, at least once in a while. But that fear can be a prod, a challenge to learn something new, to trust that God is doing something new within us, helping some new ability to grow and emerge. It didn't really hit me until graduate school, but I remember being absolutely terrified the first time I had to do a significant presentation in a graduate course. I was awake almost all night, afraid of having to speak in public before my peers. The great irony is that somehow I ended up in the business of having to do it all the time. Somehow the biggest challenges in our lives often turn into blessings.

The questions and questing that sent me to that college chapel in the middle of the night had a great deal to do with making sense of being an individual in the midst of community—how to have an appropriate pride in who I was, and not to let that disappear in relationship with other appropriately well-differentiated people. We all wrestle with how to love ourselves in the process of loving others.

I also went to that chapel seeking a relationship with something and someone beyond what I seemed to be learning as a science major. I didn't find as much of an answer as I hoped for, but it did reassure me that I wasn't alone in the midst of that searching. It wasn't until I was in graduate school, and I began to read the great physicists of the early twentieth century—Heisenberg, Bohr, Einstein—that I realized that other scientists could talk about mystery and wonder. That was the permission I needed, or the lens that validated my sense of wonder and awe in the face of the amazing beauty of creation. It was an invitation to let my faith expand and grow. It was an invitation both to vulnerability and to confidence. For each of us that invitation is connected to learning all sorts of new and challenging things.

Back to the Ascension. In order for those disciples to carry on without Rabbi Jesus, they have to take a big leap—they have to risk feeling foolish and admitting they don't know it all, and they have to try out new behaviors. The great gift is that they don't do it alone—they have a community, and they have the presence of the spirit in their midst. God is indeed with them. That's what I reliably found in the chapel at midnight. I have since learned to find that reality in other ways and in other places, so that I can be reasonably confident, most of the time, that I am beloved, that I am accompanied, even when I don't act like it or feel like it.

The Ascension is a story about the next stage on the journey toward maturity. The disciples are told to expect the confidence that comes with the Holy Spirit, and then go and take up their work in the world, as witnesses to the creative power and abiding presence of God. They never go alone, and neither do we. Christians gather with others who are seeking and searching, and help each other discover the image of the risen Jesus in the face of their neighbors, hear the voice of the spirit speaking within their own hearts and in the voices of their friends and know the abiding presence of God wherever they go. The faith community—each gathering of the Body of Christ—is perhaps the most essential character of the church, for it continually gives us the opportunity to show others—and ourselves—that we are never alone, even when we walk through the valley of the shadow of death.

Jesus's departure is critical. Those disciples won't be able to take on leadership and responsibility if they're still waiting for the Rabbi to tell them what to do. After the Ascension, they have to start working out the challenges together. Jesus reminds them that they won't be alone, and support and guidance are going to come in new ways—in a community gathered in the presence of the spirit, at home and on the road.

Making Your Mark

Where do you find companions who can offer confidence and courage? Correction or critique?

The Freedom to Serve

Have you ever been to jail—even just to visit? Many people find it pretty intimidating just to walk in there and hear the doors clang shut behind them. Even people who go in frequently notice the restrictions—you leave your keys and your ID with the guards as you enter, there are lots of other things you can't take in with you, including wine even if you're going to celebrate communion, and generally you can't touch the inmates or share any personal information. It is very clear that someone else is in control.

The disciples on that first day of the week—a week after Jesus's resurrection—have made their own prison—they've barred the doors to keep others out (John 20:19). They're living in fear of the people outside, and even though the gospel defines those people as "the Jews," the disciples are actually afraid of the religious and the political leaders in Jerusalem: the Roman government and the religious authorities who arrested and executed Jesus.

Those disciples are walled up and locked in, thanks to their fear. Jesus gets in anyway—and believe me, some days it's easier to meet Jesus in jail than it is on the outside. But Thomas misses that pastoral call, and even though his fellow inmates tell him about Jesus's visit, he asks for more evidence that Jesus has risen from the dead.

We could all do with a little more evidence. There are times in the lives of each of us when we need some physical evidence, particularly a visit from someone with "skin on."

I read a remarkable memoir about a Japanese immigrant who arrived in America with a degree in agriculture in 1916 to learn more about American farming methods. Hisanori Kano was the second son of a distinguished Japanese family who became a Christian at age eighteen, owing to the example of two classmates. He understood his journey here to the United States as a missionary one, to improve the skills of Japanese immigrants, most of whom were farmers or agriculturalists. He came with the support and advocacy of William Jennings Bryan, the notable American politician and three-time presidential candidate, whom he had met as a teenager.

In the late 1880s increasing numbers of Japanese people immigrated to the United States, particularly after the government excluded the Chinese. In 1907 our respective governments came to a so-called gentlemen's agreement that ended invitations to new workers from Japan, and in 1924 any further immigration was effectively barred. Those Japanese already here were prevented from becoming naturalized or obtaining citizenship by a law passed in 1790. Their children who were born here automatically became citizens, but the first generation was barred from that privilege. After Kano came here, many of the western states also passed laws to prevent Japanese immigrants from owning land, or even leasing substantial acreage for farming. Fear of the foreigner is not new on these shores.

By December 1941 when Kano was living and farming in Nebraska, he had married his Japanese fiancée, he had three children, and he was serving his fellow Japanese immigrants and their families as an Episcopal priest and what amounted to an agricultural extension agent. He had also spoken out in several legislative forums about discrimination against the Japanese. The night of the Pearl Harbor bombing he was arrested, and even though the bishop of Nebraska and others stood up for him, he was the only Japanese in Nebraska to be imprisoned and detained for the rest of the war.

Kano's memoir tells about how each prison or internment camp became his congregation. In the first days of the war, three German immigrants were rounded up along with him. Kano ministered to them in their despair, and helped them through the hearings that eventually ended in their release. His next stop was a military jail, where he was held with several dozen American soldiers facing court martial. As a body on the first Sunday they were there, the soldiers decided not to attend services in the base chapel, which would have given them a little bit of liberty, but instead to ask Kano to hold services for them. American soldiers, Japanese priest. Jesus got through those locked doors.

Kano was in four different lockups during the war, and after a couple of years he was released on parole, but only to house arrest. That farmer couldn't even go outside until his detention site was shifted to Nashotah House in Wisconsin—apparently the government decided he couldn't stir up too much trouble at an Episcopal seminary! All through those years he continued to preach freedom, asking his fellow detainees not to hold a grudge but to seek the well-being of their adopted nation. When others locked the doors from the outside, he responded by opening his heart. Kano continued to provide evidence of resurrection for many, many people, until he died in 1988 at the age of ninety-nine.[1]

I recently visited a congregation that sponsors a group for people whose previous religious experience has been one of spiritual abuse or imprisonment, and each parishioner there has become evidence of resurrection to those who have known religious communities as jails. Jesus's disciples didn't begin to open the cell door until they found the courage and confidence that the presence of God-with-them gave them, until they began to remember that they would find God wherever they went, even into the valley of the shadow of death.

I've also met congregations who are present with people whose jail is poverty—and that means everyone in the community, not just the identifiably poor, for when some live diminished lives because of lack of food or shelter, education or employment, we are all diminished. All of us are inmates in need of physical evidence of the risen one in our midst. How will we give evidence of the hope that is within us?

If we are really the Body of Christ, then offering evidence of the risen one is part of what it means to follow him. That is what baptism is about—when we join this body, we become part of the resurrection witness, giving evidence of our own healed wounds and resurrected life. Out of the experience of death and suffering comes hope for the new thing that God is working in us and in those around us. Consider your own life: Where have you felt abandoned, lonely, lost, or hopeless? Who helped to heal that, and how? Those German prisoners found hope through the presence of the other members of their little community, gathered to offer prayer before each one went off for his hearing, and were ready to receive the weary and angry inmate back afterward. Kano spent a lot of his time reminding his fellow prisoners to treat their captors graciously.

Not long ago, I read a news story about airline workers and how agents deal with bumped or delayed passengers. The culture of that workplace is that the customer is always treated with dignity, but the story notes that a customer who is caught up in his own infuriation is very unlikely to get special treatment. The one who finds a seat on an overbooked aircraft is more often the one who takes the situation calmly, choosing not to be imprisoned by anger. How do we offer each other hope for a way out of the chaotic mess of air travel or crossing the border to Canada or waiting in line at the department of motor vehicles? Sometimes it's the simple decision to smile and not take ourselves quite so seriously. Often it's the ability to meet others as the image of God: Oh, my! There goes Jesus in another guise!

Part of our mission as Christians is to be willing to look for the image of God in prison. As we respond to the needs around us in a spirit of loving service, we open up the prison gates and let Jesus in.

Making Your Mark

What are the prisons we see around us, in our own lives? Which of them are self-imposed?

Leading into New Waters

—⟋⟋⟋—

L et me tell you a little story about leadership. There's a small mission congregation on the Columbia River in southern Washington State, started by retired Hudson's Bay employees in the 1850s. St. James has never been very big, they've never had a full-time priest, and they've always been a mission congregation; never a full-fledged parish. In 1985 one of the members looked around at the larger community and noticed that the bottom had fallen out of the three main industries—fishing, lumbering, and dairying—and at the same time, women were moving into the workforce or going back to school, and there was no child care available. She said to the vestry, "If I can use two Sunday school rooms, and if I can find seven children, I think we can break even."

Today, the St. James Family Center is the third largest employer in the county. It provides preschool and Head Start programs that care for children from one month through age twelve; it runs teen programs, parenting programs, the county domestic violence shelter; and it has transformed the entire surrounding community. The center helps children and families develop their capacity for effective problem solving, decision making, and interpersonal relationships. The people there are a living witness to God's mission: They are instilling dignity and forming leaders, nurturing them in the faith, and helping them to recognize they are made in the image of God.

Leadership is the ability to cause others to go with you. As mentioned previously, the word for "leading" comes from German roots that mean to go, or travel, or guide. For us today it's about moving into a different future. Leaders are change agents, or encouragers into a transformed future. Since we haven't yet arrived at the fullness of the reign of God, we have some change and traveling to do before we get there, and a crucial part of that is forming leaders in the faith who will help us move toward that vision.

Here's another story about leadership. A new rector in a very comfortable suburban parish planned a mission trip to Mexico for the middle-schoolers. But by the summer of the trip, the violence in Mexico, at least at the border, was such that it no longer seemed terribly prudent to take them, so their mission locale shifted to inner city Buffalo, ten miles away. Five middle-schoolers were taken to visit a city mission, where they spent the night and helped to inventory the food pantry. When they came home they told others about staying in a "sketchy" part of town—what would they have said about the Mexican border? But the priest asked these five kids what they wanted to do in response to that visit. They asked to preach, and they started to challenge their elders about getting involved in the lives of poor people. They pushed for financial donations for the food bank and for hands-on involvement. Today that congregation helps to keep the food bank organized, and a team goes regularly to fill bags and boxes for distribution. Since the kids know what's in the food bank, they remind other parishioners to stop bringing Jell-O and start providing peanut butter and tuna fish. They prod the older members to go and meet the people who come to the food bank. Transformation is going on at all sorts of different levels.

Leadership means encouraging others to go with you—usually into unfamiliar territory. Some very particular contexts and challenges are facing us as Episcopalians today, where leaders like these are very much needed.

Our context is shifting rapidly, and it's shifting away from an Anglo, English-speaking, US-focused church, worshiping in comfortable, historic buildings with those who already know what it means to be a Christian. The fields ripe for harvest include the unchurched and those who claim their religious preference is "none of the above." For most of us, that is deeply foreign territory, but if you're under thirty it's just normal. Other fields are filled with first- and second-generation immigrants, as well as those who have rejected the religious tradition of their earlier years out of a deep sense of hurt.

The fastest-growing parts of our church are the overseas dioceses (twelve of them), immigrant congregations in the United States, and those congregations intensely focused on the needs of the communities around them. Other congregations tend to be static or shrinking—usually for a failure of leadership rather than an absence of need or a dearth of resources. Congregations who are primarily inwardly oriented are already in the throes of death, although usually in denial about it. That dying can be good news if the process is engaged appropriately. Can we encourage those congregations to think about the positive aspects of hospice care, as the dying prepare to let go of the unimportant and the non-essential? Is a large building becoming an albatross? Can it be repurposed for a different kind of mission? St. James had a large piece of land that had been given decades ago with the hope that eventually they'd be able to build a large sanctuary and move their worship out of the parish hall. Instead, they used that land to build the Family Center. Other congregations are turning their empty church school wings into weekday schools or after-school programs.

Are the congregations in a city willing to look strategically at their shared resources and the challenges of their community? I heard clergy in the rust belt recently start to talk about varying their service times to serve populations working in casinos and doing shift work—and making these changes collegially and col-lectively. Jesus did not institute the 8:00 and 10:00 a.m. Sunday morning schedule. Nor did he recruit apostles who all came from the same background or thought alike. The Body of Christ has dif-ferent gifts for a reason. Some are *not* intrinsically better than oth-ers—but some *are* better suited to particular missional challenges and not necessarily to others.

Do our structures serve our mission? Do we assume that the only valid kinds of congregations are those with their own build-ings? There is a congregation in England that had a centuries-old stone church literally falling down around their ears. They let it fall. Now the faithful meet in house churches, and every two weeks they gather for worship and a shared meal in the parish hall.

Is our vision of what's possible being limited by our boundaries? Can we nurture the faith as we collaborate with other congrega-tions to serve the larger worshiping community? Can we think even bigger, for the purposes of mission? What direction are we look-ing—inward or outward? Do we expect people to come to us, or are we willing to go out into the community to meet Jesus where he already is? Most congregations host AA meetings and other twelve-step groups, often several times a week, yet I know of only two that have seen those recovery groups as a mission field and have begun to help them nurture worshiping communities.

The challenges around us have continuity with some of the ancient ones, but we also have new realities in our increasingly post-Christian, postmodern, post-denominational North American con-text. Our increasing interfaith encounters should be understood not as a threat but as God saying, "Here are potential partnerships for mission." We are facing the most rapid and radical climate change in human history, and we're facing a widening gulf between rich and poor. At the same time, we have faster and more interconnected global communications than human beings have ever known. How are we blessing the best of those gifts for service?

All of those changing realities are opportunities for engagement in God's mission—including forming new believers. But they also scare people because they're unfamiliar. Even if my grandmother gave the church that light bulb that I would prefer not to change, perhaps I ought to be thinking about getting a CFL (compact fluorescent lamp) and a solar panel on the roof. The task of leaders is to embrace challenge as opportunity and to lead boldly where no one has gone before. That takes courage and a willingness to risk and try new things, and it takes faithfulness to a vision—that dream we call the reign of God. What did Jesus say was nonnegotiable? Love God, and love your neighbor as yourself. Rabbi Hillel said the rest of scripture was merely commentary.

We know the vision of a healed world through many different scenes and images—the garden of Eden, Isaiah's banquet on a hillside, the nations streaming to Zion, a world of justice and peace, lions lying down with lambs, the reign of God, shalom. The people of St. James understand that, and so do the kids of St. Paul's in Williamsville, New York, with the food bank. A healed world looks a little bit different in every context—what does it look like in yours?

So much of the work of leadership is about nurturing a creative and courageous response to the unfamiliar—starting with the same words that the heavenly messengers always use, "Fear not." Fear not, for God is at work in this challenging opportunity outside your door. Fear not, for Jesus is going to walk with you into a prison or a barrio or a new culture. Fear not, for the gifts you need are already present, even if you haven't discovered them yet.

All Saints in Smyrna, Tennessee, had a very painful split a number of years ago. The priest and most of the congregation left in the midst of that conflict. Those few who remained had a relatively new building, a big mortgage, and twenty acres of bottom land where they'd planned to put softball fields. They thought hard about closing and even listed the property for sale. But along came a group of refugees who'd been resettled nearby, looking for a place to worship. They were Karen people from Myanmar; they were Anglicans, and farmers. Today there are truck gardens on those bottom lands and a thriving congregation that looks very different from the original one, and speaks more than one language. They share meals, worship, and leadership. They have a Karen priest and an Anglo one.

Leadership also takes the kind of courage that is called vulnerability—whether as compassion or as recognizing that none of us has all the answers, that we have to put our trust in God and stay open to whatever comes, even when we can't quite see the road ahead. Jesus sends us; he doesn't tell us to stay where we are. Mission is about going, not staying—except staying in ongoing relationship with God and others. We are meant to be people who keep on crossing borders, because we haven't yet arrived at the fullness of the reign of God, and there are miles to go before we sleep at the last.

Our part in God's mission is to hold up the reign of God as our destination, to get up, go out there, and go after it, together with as many others as we can convince to go with us. We need leaders with courage to boldly go where we've never gone before.

This is a wonderful prayer attributed to an early Anglican explorer, Sir Francis Drake, whose chaplain held an Anglican service on the shores of the West Coast in 1579. As we take the mission journey, it's a fitting prayer for each of us as well:

> Disturb us, Lord, when we are too pleased with ourselves, when our dreams have come true because we dreamed too little, when we arrived safely because we sailed too close to the shore.
>
> Disturb us, Lord, when with the abundance of things we possess we have lost our thirst for the waters of life; having fallen in love with life, we have ceased to dream of eternity and in our efforts to build a new earth, we have allowed our vision of the new heaven to dim.

Disturb us, Lord, to dare more boldly, to venture on wilder seas where storms will show your mastery; where losing sight of the land, we shall find the stars.

We ask you to push back the horizons of our hopes; and to push back the future in strength, courage, hope, and love.

This we ask in the name of our Captain, who is Jesus.

Making Your Mark

What creative ways of forming new leaders have you found in your faith community?

PART III

The Third Mark of Mission
To Respond to Human Need with Loving Service

Salt of the Earth

Sometimes on a quiet evening in the desert, you can walk outside and smell salt. It's a whiff of what it smells like at the ocean—not as strong, but definitely salty. There has to be a little moisture in the air, but not too much. What you smell is a result of the desert rocks getting worn down and the rain dissolving the minerals out of that ground-up rock. That's ultimately where all the salts in the ocean come from, and it's also what produces dry alkali lakebeds in the desert. The process depends on sunlight as well—through the heat engine that drives the wind and erosion and evaporates the water.

The particular kind of salt that we eat and cook with has also long been associated with healing. It's a sign of hospitality in the Middle East and on the steppes of Asia—bread and salt are offered when a guest arrives, as a way of saying, "Welcome—you will be treated as a friend here."

Salt is essential to human life. A lack of salt, over a long period of time, is debilitating and even deadly. Wounds won't heal if a person is salt-deprived. People who exercise or work in the heat must replace the salt lost in sweat or they will die. A lack of iodine (usually absorbed as an iodine salt) causes both thyroid problems and mental retardation—and a third of the world's people don't get enough.

Salt is life, and salt is also a preservative. Salt cod and salted beef, and even pickles, depend on salt's ability to stop the growth of bacteria, mostly by drying out the food so much that nothing can grow on it. Salt's preservative powers make salt mines a good place to keep things safe, whether it's intrinsically dangerous stuff like nuclear waste, or precious things, like old and delicate photographic films.

Salts of all sorts are active and reactive in the presence of water—and that's a good part of what Jesus likely means when he says, "You are the salt of the earth" (Matthew 5:13). Salts can also play an important part in producing light. Think about a battery—or a firefly. Through the interaction of salts in solution, they're both ways of producing light.

When living water and the salt of the earth get together, they light up the world, and do some healing as well. That's not a bad description of motivated human beings loving their neighbors, both friends and strangers. That's even reflected in baptism in some places, where salt is added to the water of the font, or in some traditions, where a bit of salt is placed on the tongue of the newly baptized.

The same heat engine that draws salts out of the desert mountains produces the seasonal vagaries of our weather—the heat of summer and the cold of winter. Not long ago, the same arctic blast that froze pipes in the desert was pushing the temperature toward thirty below in Casper, Wyoming, where someone alerted others to the fact that the homeless people in and around town were not likely to survive a night in that kind of cold. The local Episcopal church opened its doors, advertised their intentions on Facebook, mobilized members and many others in the community to bring clothing, bedding, and food, to stay the night and offer hospitality to all comers. Radio stations advertised the emergency warming shelter and community members answered. One local businessperson who'd never been to the church before showed up, took over the kitchen, and started churning out soup, muffins, and cookies. Volunteers with clothing and food went out looking for people under bridges. One man who doesn't have a permanent home came to volunteer at the church and ended up directing others where to look for people who might be shivering in cold apartments or out in the open. Those who came to volunteer met people in need and others who wanted to help. Plans for a regular cold-weather shelter are growing out of this experience, and a new community has begun to form. That's an example of the kind of salt and light that Jesus talks about in the gospel. And it's an example of mission in action.

It's also what the Hebrew prophet Isaiah is quite literally talking about: sharing bread with the hungry, and bringing the homeless into your house. Do that, says the prophet, and your light will shine forth like the dawn, and healing will spring up quickly (Isaiah 58:8).

There are any number of faith communities who know firsthand about salt and light. The after-school program at St. Philip's Church in Tucson is a great example. The kids who participate get fed physically and spiritually, in ways that help them become light sources for others—through their singing and music-making, and through the harmony they bring into their relationships far beyond the walls of the church. Healing grows and spreads from that salt and light.

There are other kinds of salts that we don't often think about so positively, like iron oxide, or rust. But consider how its ability to eat away the metal of prison bars or destroy instruments of war might help to create more light in this world. The corrosive power of salt is not always destructive. There's a reflection of that reality in the sense of salty words—those words that can stop conversations, or the ones our mothers tried to stop us using with a bar of soap. They're connected to the challenging words of the prophets, and to Jesus's insistence that he's not going to let go of those words. Hear the words of the prophet Isaiah: "Loose the bonds of injustice, let the oppressed go free, break all the yokes that keep people in thrall, share your bread with the hungry, bring the homeless into your house, cover the naked, care for your own kin in need. Do that, and your light will shine out like the dawn" (cf. Isaiah 58:6–8).

What sort of salty work or words does our world need? I heard the lament about guns and violence everywhere I went in Arizona after the shooting of Congresswoman Gabrielle Giffords and others in January 2011. That wound is raw and open, and it needs deep and penetrating balm. It will take the abrasive salt of challenge to power structures that keep on saying, "Guns don't kill people, people do." Well, fewer people die if guns aren't readily available in every other purse or glove box. Reducing their availability will take entire communities working together, and it won't happen in an instant. Change will take something like the persistent work of rust.

The work of healing from violence will be like that heat engine, slowly eroding salt from the mountains and dissolving it in raindrops, and it will need many kinds of salts—like years of after-school programs slowly loving kids into healthier adults. Healing will need a greater investment in the health of our neighbors, and the willingness to intervene when someone is deathly ill, whether from the likelihood of freezing to death in the cold or from acute mental illness. Healing will come from nurturing communities of light to challenge the violence of words that assume that some people aren't worth knowing or listening to. Every member of every human community is of immense value—our part in God's mission is to break those bonds, even if it takes the rust of years to do it.

Communities of faith have abundant resources of salt. We can hasten healing with our sweat and our rusty persistence and our salty tears. Our labors will transform those tears into tears of joy, as the light begins to shine more brightly. We are the salt of the earth. We are the light of the world. The work of mission is to let it shine.

Making Your Mark

How have salt and light played a part in your response to human need?

Face to Face

What is a face? The Book of Genesis tells us that God created plants for food—and that's all. Some people won't eat anything that has a face, which usually means warm-blooded animals. Some won't eat birds, or frogs, or fish.

What does a face imply about something that has one? Probably something about awareness, and maybe the ability to feel or suffer. To most people, a face means "animal." Yet plants have awareness, and even something like a great expanse of fungi or mycorrhizae has the ability to sense a threat and seek to avoid it. Plants are aware in ways that we human beings don't always recognize. What is it that keeps a sunflower turning to face the sun all through the day, and even through the hours of darkness, so that its face is poised to receive the first rays of the rising sun?

"In the beginning when God created the heavens and the earth, the earth was a formless void and darkness covered the face of the deep, while a wind from God swept over the face of the waters" (Genesis 1:1–2). What does it mean for the deep or the waters to have a face?

God's spirit acts on the deep expanse of waters in such a way that the waters respond. God speaks, and the light emerges. God speaks, and the dome separates the waters beneath from the waters above. God speaks, and the waters gather into seas.

A face has something to do with the ability to respond, and, in Genesis, to respond to the word of God. We even use the word for parts of creation that we normally think of as inanimate. A rock face, like Half Dome in Yosemite, or Stone Face Rock near Pennington Gap, is the part of the mountain that responds to the forces of change like wind and water and ice. It is the part that relates to the rest of the world.

Look around at your neighbors' faces. What do these faces imply?

A face is also what we define as distinctive about our understanding of God. When our Greek forebears in the faith began to speak of God as Trinity, and note that the Trinity has three persons, they used a word—*prosopon*—that means both person and face. We say that human beings are made in the image of God, that they bear, in some way, the face of God. We say that Jesus is the human face of God. We speak of meeting God face to face—at the end of life or the last judgment, but also in the sense of turning toward the Divine, or in recognizing the presence of God in creation, in Jesus our brother, or in the spirit who continues to inspire us.

In some real sense we cannot meet God except by facing and turning toward the Divine with that relational part of ourselves that engages another person. We cannot love our neighbors without facing toward them, without recognizing the image of God in their being. Nor can we love ourselves without seeing God's beloved reflected in the mirror.

We need faces in order to build relationships. We have to recognize something familiar in order to start relationships, which is why babies and their parents spend so much time looking at each other. Babies begin to trust that this mother or father face will provide food and comfort and incarnate love, and those babies can only thrive when there is some predictability to the faces around them.

We learn to love through trusting a face, and in the process of maturing, our own faces become trustworthy. That is a great part of what it means to grow up into the full stature of Christ (Ephesians 4:13)—to become a predictable and faithful representation of the loving face of God.

When a face changes, we don't always recognize it easily. I saw a face across the room recently, thought I recognized it, but I wasn't sure that it was my friend from over twenty years ago until he came closer—he'd changed a lot. Something like that is going on with the disciples at Easter. Mary Magdalene and the other Mary have been to the tomb, met and recognized Jesus. He instructs them to tell the others to go to Galilee and meet him there. But when they get there and see Jesus, they don't all recognize him. His face has changed in some way. Some worship him, and some aren't sure who he is. But he tells them to go and teach the whole world about what he has taught them.

What would we teach? What does the trustworthy face of Jesus convey to us? Perhaps, "You are my friends; love each other as I have loved you. By this everyone will know that you are my disciples, if you have love for one another" (John 15:12–17, my summary) or as Matthew's gospel puts it, "Lord, when was it that we saw you hungry and gave you food, or thirsty and gave you something to drink? And when was it that we saw you a stranger and welcomed you, or naked and gave you clothing? And when was it that we saw you sick or in prison and visited you?" And the king will answer them, "Truly I tell you, just as you did it to one of the least of these who are members of my family, you did it to me" (Matthew 25:37–40).

What does the trustworthy face of God look like, particularly in those who bear God's image on their own faces? The world yearns for faces that can be trusted, faces that bear a message of beloved welcome, that send news of solidarity, even in the midst of trouble.

An Episcopal priest serving a congregation in Cairo, Egypt, during the upheavals in early 2011 wrote about the religious violence there that the news media had reported as clashes between fundamentalist Muslims and Christians. He told a more nuanced story of a handful of Christian women seeking to escape violent marriages, who had no ability to divorce, and found a way to leave those marriages by converting to Islam. Brothers and husbands and fathers were taking revenge on those who welcomed these women, and others were retaliating. Churches, homes, and shops were being destroyed. Yet the surrounding community of Muslims and Christians took to the streets in demonstrations of support for one another. The priest told of shrouded Muslim women in full veils marching down the streets, with crosses painted on their veils. They cannot show their faces in public, but they can demonstrate their support and solidarity.

That's also what's needed in Sudan—people searching for trustworthy friends, and acting like trustworthy, loving neighbors in the face of suspicion and mistrust that moves toward armed violence. Jesus's response is always about nonviolent witness, to say that I will love you even if you attack and persecute me. Yet he doesn't tell people just to lie down and die. Solidarity with others brings a bolder face, maybe something like a fish or butterfly that bears great big eyes on its sides or wings. Those eyes aren't full faces, but they convince predators: Don't attack this face, for a much larger creature is looking back at you. They turn away predators by bearing witness to something larger than themselves. That is what the Body of Christ is meant to be—not threatening, but reassuring and bearing the eternal confidence that nothing can keep this body down forever. It will rise again, for God will keep on doing a new thing, even when the world's evil strikes the body down.

The tyrants have already been put on notice that the world is watching. We stand with our brothers and sisters in Sudan, facing the violence, turning our faces toward Jerusalem, and saying an eternal "NO!" to forces that would deny or diminish life. We stand with our brothers and sisters through the yet unfinished Arab Spring. We can do no less—mission is to respond to suffering with loving service. The Body of Christ will live only if together we can turn our faces toward the light.

Making Your Mark

Think about the ways you've come face-to-face with God in your own community. How has that experience influenced your response to serve others?

Healing and Wholeness

The work of clergy has anciently been called the "cure of souls" and in some places, a cleric's locus of work is still called a "cure." Pastoral ministry is focused on the care of human beings, "soul" being shorthand for the whole person, even if that shorthand has been forgotten in some times and places. Cure and care are intimately related, including their origin in words that mean "to have concern for," or even "lament" or "grieve." Cure and care are equally the focus of the medical world. In recent decades we've seen an expanding recognition that cure and care have to do with far more than the remission of acute symptoms in a particular body part. There have been strands in both religious and medical traditions that have understood healing to be about a larger vision, but they haven't always been seen as the avowed purpose, or the public center, of either tradition.

Healing is directly related to health and wholeness, and to holiness. In English those words all come from the same root and have to do with continuing in, or moving toward, a desired state of being, something more closely approximating perfection or completeness. The Abrahamic religious traditions uphold a vision for the healing of all that is, human beings individually as well as in community, their relationships to the Divine, and the relationships among all the various parts of creation. That vision is variously called *tikkun olam* (the repair of the world), shalom, salvation, or the reign of God. "Shalom" in Hebrew, or "salaam" in Arabic, is a kind of shorthand for that prophetic dream of a healed world, and it underlies the ancient prophetic insistence on the need for multiple forms of healing, leading to a world of justice and peace. That dream includes the healing of individuals as well as communities and nations and insists that all have access to the blessings of life—food and adequate abundance for a feast, shelter from the elements as well as war and violence, and the kind of health that lets each one live an active life, productive and full of years. That vision insists that right relationship with the earth and the rest of creation, as well as the divine origin of all those blessings, is part of that overarching dream.

Salvation may seem like an unduly loaded theological word for that concept, but at its root it also means healing—and the etymological connections are far more evident in the romance languages than they are in English. The Syriac church in Baghdad that was bombed recently is named Our Lady of Salvation; its French name is Notre Dame de Salud—"Our Lady of Health." That word is as much about health and wholeness as it is about rescue. Salvation at its deepest and most eternal is beyond any narrow understanding of soul as somehow separate from the rest of a human person, or an individual disconnected from community.

This dream of a healed world, offering health and wholeness to all humanity, underlies many religious traditions *and* medical care. Our respective goals overlap, at the very least. We are natural and appropriate partners in the healing endeavor, seeking healing for all. When we begin to look at the causes of health in human beings, we also quickly see that the health of political systems and ecosystems are major contributors, and a robustly healthy human community is intrinsically impossible in their absence.

Let's start with the immediate and local. What do we know about the role of spiritual care in treating disease, or in supporting health? Broad-based epidemiological studies show that people who participate regularly in worship, attend gatherings of faith communities, and have an underlying system of meaning in their lives enjoy better overall health, tend to do better in response to the challenge of disease, and live longer than those who lack such assets. Provision for spiritual care has been a required part of federally funded hospice care for many years. It should be regular practice to query patients about their spiritual systems, community of support, and their desire for access to spiritual care. Caring for the whole person requires this as best practice, and it is an essential part of the Hippocratic Oath.

Medical care providers themselves benefit from spiritual communities that support meaning-making in the face of life and death decisions. How and where do doctors and nurses find the inner resources when they've signed too many death certificates or delivered too many terminal diagnoses? Their own full humanity—and health—requires making some connection to larger questions of meaning. Most are drawn into the healing arts out of wonder at the human body and its capacities, or out of a desire to help others—or both. Those motivations partake of transcendence—connection to something bigger than an individual—and both are nourished and encouraged to grow and deepen in company with others who share an understanding of being part of something larger and lasting.

Another significant place of connection is ethical reflection. We need to consider whether approaches and protocols are not only doable, but *should* be done. Even when entire communities are unlikely to reach consensus on approaches and protocols, we need to have the conversations and explore the parameters. That work can help patients and families to make informed decisions congruent with their own values and beliefs in time of crisis.

Much of the intensive work of ethics committees focuses on the local—what should be done in this case, with this forty-seven-year-old male with acute leukemia, or this ninety-year-old female with a broken hip and advanced dementia? But how often do we shift the focus of our lens to the larger community and its health? How much ethical reflection focuses on the ability of an entire hospital system to improve health, or the choices a medical practice will consider in treating severe birth anomalies in a heavily industrialized area? These are not decisions that should be left solely to "management." Communities of ethical discourse can encourage management to shift its gaze—at least in part—toward issues of health in the larger community, and the religious community can be a significant partner in that expansive work. If we are to heal the larger body, then questions of purpose, vision, and mission must be engaged. It is a responsibility shared by the healing communities of both faith and medicine.

Consider some of those larger community health issues—the vastly increased incidence of asthma in poor inner-city environments, or the rates of type 2 diabetes in the same places, often called "food deserts"—that is, neighborhoods where wholesome, affordable food is unavailable. We're beginning to see rising rates of diabetes in India, as a result of a different but connected problem—sudden access to improved diets. Women in India have borne small and relatively poorly nourished babies for generations.[1] When those children become adults with access to richer diets, they are far more susceptible to diabetes, and at younger ages, than their poorer relatives and ancestors. Native Americans live with a similar problem: The available food is overly processed and nutritionally skewed from the historic range of foodstuffs. Does the responsibility of the health care community extend beyond treating the individual diabetes patient? Does the responsibility of a pastor go beyond praying with a sick person and ensuring that she has transportation to her medical appointments? The epidemic won't be healed by addressing the intensely local issue, as necessary as that is. The sickness of God's people is a systemic illness that says that only some deserve access to education, healthy foods, and early medical treatment. The global disease is about how resources are shared or not shared, and it includes a skewed vision of what a healed world looks like. That primal vision is neither an eternal orgy of over-consumption nor soul-killing deprivation.

Neither does it envision a world where people eat anything in sight because they are bored or depressed, or consume junk calories because truly good food is unavailable.

Part of our mission is to respond to human disease by proclaiming, advertising, and teaching about what health really looks like. That vision of health must include both the particular and the general, the individual and communal, and it must include hope for health among those with "disabilities" or "disease." That may be where the nature of the spiritual teacher becomes most essential. The Abrahamic traditions share a broad understanding of what perfection is and is not. Elements of each tradition understand that healing is possible in the process of dying, as well as in the small dyings that are part of every human life. Grief or loss can produce a more engaged and rewarding life once the loss begins to heal. That does not deny the gift of the life, or the part of life, that has been lost, but it does affirm that healing is always possible. Hope—not necessarily for physical cure, but for the ability to live a full and meaningful life—is an essential part of healing and of wholeness.

That shift in outlook from despair toward hope is foundational to healing the whole. It may also be an essential shift in improving basic medical care. I had a fascinating conversation recently with a professor who works on safety and medical errors. We quickly began to focus on the complex environments in which we both work, and the need for adaptive leadership rather than technical fixes. Those technical fixes in hospital safety don't seem to have produced the kinds of results expected—in many contexts, error rates have not changed in ten years. What's needed is a shift in focus from the very local to the more global—in the same way that healing a patient is more likely if one addresses the whole person. Some habits and behaviors need changing—hand washing, use of checklists in the operating room, electronic charting—but even when people know what's needed, local cultures militate against those changes. Consider the difference in the culture between pilots and the medical community. It's fascinating to recognize that cockpit checklists work and are well used.

Why the difference? Is medicine a far more complex environment? Or is there a different kind of need to shift the focus to the larger goal? Is there investment in a larger-picture cultural change that insists on healing rather than fixing? Is there sufficient time for practitioners, rather than only managers, to think proactively and strategically? Significant strides in aviation safety were made when regulators began to look at accidents systemically. The National Transportation Safety Board investigates all aircraft incidents and accidents, reports publicly, studies the results over time, and as a result the Federal Aviation Authority changes its safety education for pilots. Why the differences in system-wide reporting and accountability between aviation and medicine? I don't have the answer, but it is an intriguing problem that may hold some of the seeds needed for more global kinds of healing.

As challenging as it is to build a healthier health-care system across this nation, global wholeness—a healed world—can be even more intimidating to the psyche and spirit of healers. The need and the diagnosis are overwhelming and the response has too often been spiritual or developmental paralysis. We observe World AIDS Day on December 1, and over thirty years into this pandemic, there are thirty-four million people living with HIV, 2.7 million new infections a year, and significantly underfunded prevention and drug treatment efforts.[2]

Yet even in the face of wretched international health statistics, there is much hope. We have begun to think globally about health—not just about individual diseases, but about many of the complicating and contributing factors in health. The United Nations Millennium Development Goals (MDGs), committed to by governments and engaged and promoted by faith communities, represent a shift toward global goal-setting *and* addressing underlying factors.

The MDGs grew out of economic modeling and sociological and epidemiological studies toward the end of the last century. Progress in addressing the worst of the world's sickness and poverty was being made in some areas, yet there was little coherent focus on particular issues, and little ongoing attempt to measure input and response. After economic projections showed that a relatively small contribution by the developed nations of the world would likely go a long way toward healing some of that dis-ease, people of faith began to rally support. A partnership between developed and developing nations at the turn of the millennium committed the wealthy to dedicate a specific portion of their national economic output to targeted foreign aid and the developing nations to build their capacity to receive such aid in accountable ways. That charter for healing challenged all parties to measure and benchmark our collective progress toward specific goals in a short fifteen years. We're fast approaching that date, and while we've seen some progress, we have a long way to go.

The MDGs set out eight focused areas of progress in healing, and while they apply specifically to developing nations, equivalent conditions exist in parts of the developed world: our inner cities, Native American reservations, poor and depopulating rural areas. Learnings from one sphere are often translatable to another.

The MDGs focus on the mission of healing the worst of global poverty, caring for those in need through major reductions in hunger, preventable disease, and child and maternal mortality; by improving the lot of women; by ensuring general access to primary education, sanitation, and potable water; and by developing partnerships for sustainable development.

We're making progress, and the overall rate of abject poverty will likely fall to about 15 percent, or 900 million, by 2015, from 1.4 billion today.[3]

Basic education is an essential tool. More children are going to school, particularly in the poorest countries, yet poor girls in almost all developing nations have less access to education than do boys, and rural children are twice as likely to be out of school as those in urban areas. A primary education cuts the likelihood of contracting HIV by half. Lack of access to education for girls perpetuates high adolescent birth rates and high rates of maternal and child mortality.

That peripartum mortality is slowly being alleviated by improved access to trained health workers, and child mortality is falling as well. Yet neither goal is on track to be met by 2015. More than one-third of childhood mortality is the result of malnutrition. A quarter of children in the developing world are underweight, even though there has been progress since 1990.

Empowering women improves the lives of whole communities. Around the globe, women still do more of the labor, and receive less income, than men. Women have less access to capital, and globally own only 1 percent of property. Fewer women than men have access to senior-level or political positions, though there is slow improvement. Healing requires changed power dynamics—as anyone who's studied the epidemiology of AIDS can attest.

Treating preventable disease, especially AIDS, tuberculosis, and malaria, is doable with enough money. As a global community, we spend about a quarter of what is necessary to treat and prevent AIDS, and the outlook is not encouraging. Though the infection rate is declining, the portion of HIV-positive persons in treatment is not keeping pace with new infections, and the global economic situation means it is unlikely to in the near future. We are making progress on malaria, with rapidly growing rates of bed-net use in some parts of sub-Saharan Africa. The worldwide goal for tuberculosis reduction has been met, though it's still the next major killer after AIDS.

Some of the healing work is about basic hygiene. Most regions of the world are on target to meet their potable water goals, but nearly half the developing world's population lacks adequate sanitation, and those numbers are growing. Slum conditions are slowly improving, but improvement is not keeping pace with the rising number of people living in them, and violent conflict is a significant contributor.

International aid for all of this work has increased, though not proportionally in Africa. In total, it's still less than half of what developed nations committed in 2000. These global statistics are striking, graphic, and challenging. There are similar realities here in the United States. Those challenges are systemic injustices and epidemiological realities, but only a partnership of many healers can begin to address them.

Another important element is violence. The death and destruction in Our Lady of Health/Salvation in Baghdad shares roots with the epidemic of fistulas (both as a result of rape and the lack of access to skilled health workers during childbirth) in many war-torn parts of Africa, and with suicide rates on Native American reservations and homicides in Chicago. Healers must attend to that violence. It's a symptom of grievous dis-ease, and it can only be addressed by shifting our gaze to the level of communities.

An organization called CeaseFire in Chicago is treating gang violence as an epidemic, teaching children and young people not to pass on violent behavior, and promoting immunity to violence in the wider community. It connects several kinds of healers and healing: the criminal justice system, faith leaders, public education, youth workers, and hospitals. It teaches healing techniques like conflict mediation, interrupting violence, and non-violent responses.

We are beginning to see remarkable partnerships between philanthropists, medical practitioners, communities of faith, entrepreneurs, the academy, and governments to heal the world. Fulfilling the mission to respond to those in need through loving service will take many of us, working together, to begin to bring a vision of a healed world to reality, yet our own health and survival ultimately depend on our willingness to expand the mission of care from individuals to communities, from nations to the world.

Making Your Mark

How is the community you live in affected by connections between health, systemic injustice, and violence? How might your faith community respond?

City on a Hill

Not long ago, The Episcopal Church's church-wide staff gathered in New York, from across the world: one who works from Panama, another from Scotland, and from offices in Los Angeles, Austin, Seattle, Miami, Washington, DC, as well as New York, plus individuals who work from North Carolina, Wisconsin, Minnesota, and Puerto Rico. Once a year these staff members gather for learning and team-building. The first morning we sent everyone out to visit community ministries sponsored by Episcopal churches around the New York metro area—programs that feed and shelter people, a chaplaincy in a correctional facility, after-school tutoring, senior lunches—all of them ways of healing the brokenness in the world around us. Each offers an example of what the biblical prophets talk about—giving sight to the blind and delivering prisoners, literally and figuratively. These various outposts of care and healing are light to the nations, giving glory to God, in the way envisioned by Isaiah:

> The Spirit of the Lord God is upon me,
> because the Lord has anointed me
> to bring good news to the poor;
> he has sent me to bind up the brokenhearted,
> to proclaim liberty to the captives,
> and the opening of the prison to those who are bound;
> to proclaim the year of the Lord's favor,
> and the day of vengeance of our God;
> to comfort all who mourn;

to grant to those who mourn in Zion—
to give them a beautiful headdress instead of ashes,
the oil of gladness instead of mourning,
the garment of praise instead of a faint spirit;
that they may be called oaks of righteousness,
the planting of the Lord, that he may be glorified.

(61:1–3)

People came back absolutely transformed—several people wanted to get personally involved, give money, volunteer, figure out how to do something similar in their own communities. We saw what Isaiah and Jesus speak of—human beings loving one another and giving glory to God. The second-century Christian theologian, Irenaeus, said that the glory of God is a human being fully alive, and as people returned we saw a room filled with that kind of glory.

These staff members spend their working lives supporting others who do similarly transformative ministry, but not all of them get to see it in the flesh—particularly the people who work in the finance department, or the mailroom, or in information systems or building maintenance. Even the mission department staff usually only get to see ministries that have to do with their own particular area. But it takes the whole team to help support the work of sending missionaries, linking new Latino congregations with Christian education resources in Spanish, resettling refugees, or helping congregations find new clergy. All of us, working together, become the beacon spreading light to those who live in darkness. All of us, working together, take part in God's mission to respond to human need by loving service. Whenever we feed hungry people, or shelter the homeless, or provide warm coats for little kids who don't have any, we are light to the nations.

Jesus uses some striking imagery for the mission of caring: "You are the light of the world. A city built on a hill cannot be hid" (Matthew 5:14). That's not so different from other great prophetic images of the city of peace—the banquet on a hill, the lion lying down with the lamb, or a city where children can play in the streets while their elders watch from park benches (Zechariah 8:4–5). The work of faith communities gives flesh to those dreams.

Building that city on a hill to be a light to the nations mostly happens by doing what Jesus asks of his friends: "Love one another as I have loved you" (John 13:34, my translation). There seems to be no end of sobering reminders of the world's desperate need for that kind of love. Consider, for example, the people of South Sudan who are seeking a nation where they no longer struggle with their neighbors over oil and borders, where they can send their children to school and expect them to grow and play and thrive. The 2011 referendum to separate from northern Sudan was remarkably peaceful, thanks in large part to the religious leaders in South Sudan, including Archbishop Daniel Deng Bul, who helped to keep it so. In spite of the referendum and a relatively peaceful separation, the new nation continues to face many challenges.

For the people of Haiti it's been several years since their nation suffered enormous death and devastation in a massive earthquake. They have a long way to go in recovery and rebuilding, but their brothers and sisters around the world stand ready to help. The Episcopal Church is engaged in a campaign to help rebuild the cathedral center, which included schools for children, a trade school, a music school, as well as Cathédrale de Sainte Trinité, that it, too, may once again be a light of God's love to the people of that land. The art in that cathedral was revolutionary when it was painted nearly sixty years ago. Most of those murals, which showed the great stories of the Bible in a Haitian context, were destroyed, but the three remaining ones are being removed and restored by the Smithsonian Institution, so that they can be returned when the cathedral is rebuilt. Light to the nation in that context also looks like pride in a nation's culture, a way to say that God loves us enough to show up right here—and Jesus looks like a Haitian! It is the eternal good news of God-is-with-us. Each one of us can share in that work of rebuilding the city on a hill, in stone and art and human dignity. Healing can happen in as many ways as there are broken human beings and relationships on this planet.

Love one another as I have loved you. That love is urgently needed as children, adults, and communities seek some shred of solace and healing from violence and poverty. Each and every city and community on this planet is meant to be a source of God's healing love. There have been abundant signs of loving others as God loves us, even to giving one's life for another, or going into the valley of the shadow of death for the sake of one in desperate need. In the aftermath of the shootings in Tucson, Arizona, that took the life of several people and grievously wounded Congresswoman Gabrielle Giffords, consider these signs of God's love: the man who sheltered his wife and died in the process; the aide who staunched the bleeding of Congresswoman Giffords; the two people who stopped the gunman from further killing. Yet it is the work of rebuilding the city that will require a longer and more intense and sacrificial focus in the days and years to come. How will each one of us love both the wounded and the wounder in Arizona? How will we shine light in the aftermath of war in Sudan, or the poverty and devastation in Haiti? How will we make peace with our neighbors next door?

The city of light to the nations is built day by day, as we love as Jesus loved, answering the hungers and hurts of the world: feeding the hungry, healing the sick, restoring the lost, freeing the prisoners of poverty and mental illness, and loving the unloved—which is what forgiveness is all about. Our light to the nations flames forth, one loving act at a time. May each of us burn brightly.

Making Your Mark

What do we do in our own faith communities to live out this healing mission? How are we giving glory to God?

Many Gifts, One Mission

M ark is the shortest of the four canonical gospels, and the fastest moving. Most scholars believe that his gospel ended abruptly: "They said nothing to anyone, for they were afraid." Clearly the women who went to the tomb on that first Easter morning did speak up, and relatively soon, or we wouldn't know about the resurrection at all. The women found their courage and their voices and went and found the others. Where were Peter and the other disciples? Hiding in an upper room—something that was probably very prudent, but not terribly bold. The women had gone to the tomb to care for the body of their dead friend and rabbi. The men went off to find a safe place and figure out what to do now that their leader was dead.

In most cultures, women are the ones who care for the bodies of loved ones. They do the kinds of intimate and personal ministry that strangers won't—like feeding and healing, massaging, nursing children, washing the bodies of the dead—and the bodies of those who are too young or too old and frail to do it for themselves. They sit with the sick and watch over them through the night. Men are capable of all those kinds of caring, even if they don't do them often. There are even a few documented cases of men producing milk and nursing babies.

When I was in the Congo recently, I visited a ministry for orphans and women who had been raped. The woman who began the work told us about finding a woman who hadn't borne a child recently, who was willing to take a drug to start her lactation and nurse an orphaned infant. She was clearly doing what Paul talks about—extending hospitality to strangers—and doing it in a deeply intimate and significant way (Romans 12:13; also Hebrews 13:2).

Much of our understanding of the gifts of women is culturally defined. We expect that women do certain things and that men do other things, and none of us finds it easy to imagine people in unexpected roles.

But Jesus himself confronts those cultural boundaries. He speaks with women in public, which was highly inappropriate in his culture. He teaches them, which was also taboo. There's a first-century pronouncement that says that to teach your daughter Torah (the Hebrew Bible) is like making her a harlot. But Jesus doesn't hesitate.

Jesus praises the woman who washes his feet with her tears and wipes them with her hair, saying that she is caring for his body before it's buried. When Martha complains about her sister Mary not doing her share of work in the kitchen, Jesus basically says, that's not a problem: "Mary has chosen the better part" (Luke 10:42).

The good news of Jesus is for all people, without distinction. When Paul insists that in Christ there is neither Jew nor Greek, slave nor free, male and female (Galatians 3:28), he is reminding us that in the Body of Christ the world's cultural distinctions don't matter. We are all members of the body, with particular gifts to be used for the good of the whole world. If we think about roles today, we might say, if a woman wants to study, so be it; if she wants to sew or farm or pilot a plane or design bridges, thank God; if a man wants to be a nurse, encourage him; if a man wants to look after children, give thanks, for there are far more children needing care than there are adults who are willing. God needs the gifts of all of us in order to heal this broken and suffering world.

In his letter to the Romans, Paul says, "Love one another with mutual affection ... serve the Lord ... extend hospitality to strangers" (Romans 12:10–13). Are we willing to love each other, serve God with what God has given us, and be hospitable, even if we discover that familiar people have unexpected gifts?

On a visit to the African nation of Zambia, we had several very vigorous discussions about women's ordination. The bishops there have no theological objection, but they have wanted to wait for others who are troubled by the idea. The clergy of one diocese complained that they had never talked about ordaining women. I told them that now that they had seen one, they had an excuse to go home and talk about it. What keeps us from seeing possibilities in others? What limits our eyesight?

The Orthodox churches of the East call Mary Magdalene the first apostle, the apostle to the apostles, because she was the first to proclaim the resurrection. Proclaiming the resurrection is a task we all share—and so is the work of caring for bodies. We cannot love God and love our neighbors as ourselves without doing both. The mission of the gospel is about caring for the whole person, as God cares for the whole creation. It also takes the whole church, the whole Body of Christ, to serve the whole of that gospel.

Jesus anoints, massages, and touches people to heal them. He goes to the bedside of the dying and dead, and he comforts the grieving. He soothes his frightened disciples in a storm-tossed boat, like a mother comforting children having a bad dream. And to this day Jesus feeds us from his own body. Around the year 1100, Anselm, the archbishop of Canterbury, called Jesus our mother for that very reason. That may seem shocking—but then so is the incarnation, the daring reality that God would take on human flesh.

God's work among us is not limited to any race or language or people. God's work is not limited to either gender. God's work is the work of caring, feeding, teaching, and healing both individual human beings and entire nations.

God's dream of a healed world needs us all. It is not our job to say where or in whom God plants gifts—for they are God's gifts, not our own possession. But it is our task—our part in God's mission—to celebrate and hold fast to what is good in those gifts and skills and encourage their use for the good of the whole.

We are here to care for the body, and to care for the soul, and to proclaim God's dream for a healed world. Together, in the power of the spirit, we can begin to bring that dream to reality. The gifts of all God's children must be put to work for the healing of this world.

Making Your Mark

What unexpected gifts have you discovered in others—and in yourself? How have you seen these gifts used for the good of others?

The Meaning
of Mercy

—⟋⟍⟍—

Is Tyler Clementi our neighbor? How about Imam Feisal Abdul Rauf, who tried to build a Muslim cultural center in Manhattan, near Ground Zero in 2009? And while we're at it, how about Pastor Terry Jones, of the Dove World Outreach Center, who thought it was a good idea to burn Qur'ans?

I think the fate of Mr. Clementi is probably the toughest for all of us. He committed suicide out of shame, after his college roommates treated him like a zoo animal rather than a human being with basic human dignity and rights. Several other young gay people have killed themselves recently—not in such public or appallingly cruel circumstances, but for similar reasons.

The fellow on the road to Jericho—whose story is known to us in Jesus's parable of the Good Samaritan—was also treated in an appalling way, as an exploitable substance, rather than a dignified human being. He was robbed, stripped, beaten, and left for dead (Luke 10:29–37). We don't know exactly what the robbers were after, but it was something valuable. Three guys in Brooklyn suffered something similar not long ago—they were abducted, stripped, beaten, tortured, and dumped, because their tormentors thought they "had broken the rules." Those rules apparently say that you have no dignity or expectation of life if you're gay.

Exactly the same kind of attitude and behavior resulted in the lynching of several thousand African Americans, Mexicans, Chinese, and a few Anglos in the century after the Civil War. The same kind of sin continues to result in the rape and murder of countless women and men in the Congo and surrounding areas today. Similar mayhem went on in Rwanda and during the civil wars in Liberia and Sudan when millions of human beings were simply slaughtered.

Who is our neighbor? Who is being left for dead by the side of the road? Sometimes it's our collective neglect, rather than active persecution, that causes the end of other people's dignity. Think of all the people whose ability to survive has been mortally threatened by the economic crisis of the last couple of years—and people whose job skills have been going stale for a long time. The city of Detroit has been dying a slow death for decades. You may not live in Michigan, but are the residents of Detroit your neighbors? The other old industrial cities in the United States and Europe are filled with human beings also being left by the side of the road.

The Samaritan didn't just take pity on the dying man in the ditch. He gave first aid, picked him up and carted him to an inn, nursed him through the night, and then paid the innkeeper to look after him until he was well enough to go on his way. Jesus and the lawyer in the story call that mercy. Mercy recognizes a hurting human being and shares in that suffering enough to do something about it. Pity, on the other hand, is a kind of distant sorrow that doesn't take any personal responsibility.

I had a remarkable conversation recently with a couple of college students. One of them asked a very provocative question about how anyone could recognize the breadth of the world's suffering and hold onto all of it. I don't think anybody can, all the time. We have to focus on one part at a time, the suffering that's most present to us or in which our attention is demanded. As individuals, we simply aren't capable of holding it all. Even when we grow in our capacity for compassion, we have to keep traveling around, moving our attention from one situation to another. Yet together, the Body of Christ can hold all that suffering. Together, we can focus deeply on all the half-dead along the side of the road.

The question isn't just, "Who is our neighbor?" as the lawyer in the story of the Good Samaritan asked Jesus. The question is also, "How do we become more neighborly, and more able to respond?" Again, together we have far more capacity to notice the one who needs mercy, and open our hearts to respond.

That's what shared awareness, particularly in the sense of seeing a bigger view, is all about—it can lead all of us to act with greater mercy. The gospel story is named after the Samaritan, but the inn-keeper was a vital part of that merciful intervention too. The entire Episcopal Church has been asked to show mercy to Haiti in the very concrete form of millions of dollars to start reconstructing the many buildings lost in the earthquake. Mercy for the Haitian people includes schools, churches, health clinics—the infrastructure of com-passion, just like the inn where the beaten man made his recovery.

Episcopalians and other Christians frequently repeat a baptismal promise to seek and serve Christ in all persons, loving our neighbor as ourselves. It takes all of us to love all people—none of us can do it alone. The question of the Muslim cultural center in Lower Manhat-tan—and the very fact that there is a question about it—can only be addressed by the larger community of compassion. As soon as voices are raised insisting that *those people* don't deserve the same dignity as we enjoy, it's become a large-picture problem. No one of us can apply sufficient mercy to heal it. Together we can challenge our neighbors whose fear has begun to turn to hate, together we can insist that free-dom of religion applies to all of us, together we can work to reverse the prejudice that says some people can't have a place in this nation. That's the kind of mercy that Tyler Clementi needed—the same dig-nity that we accord all other teenagers, and probably an extra dose of compassion for kids who are struggling to understand their own identity, responsibility, self-worth, and indeed, belovedness.

So what about those neighbors who seem so much harder to love, like Tyler's two roommates, or the Qur'an-burning Pastor Jones? They deserve our compassion, too, along with a request for accountability.

Loving our neighbors as ourselves is about accountability, whether it's a lack of self-respect or the arrogant sense that I am the only person who matters. Tyler Clementi was shamed to death, and that has something to do with the inability of people around him to assure him that he was loved and filled with dignity because he was a child of God. His roommates evidently didn't have an adequate sense of self-love, either, if they had to look for it in shaming somebody else. Pastor Jones seems to need a similar level of community boundary setting, a willingness to say that if we're going to live together in a reasonably harmonious society, then certain kinds of disrespect are off limits.

Mercy takes many forms—and that's probably what most distinguishes it from pity. Mercy recognizes and respects incarnate reality—that this suffering is different from that suffering over there—and mercy responds appropriately to each. Around the church, and around the world, I have seen mercy becoming real. Children are being nurtured, the dead are given a final resting place, the hungry are fed—in body and soul, the wandering are helped back onto a fruitful path, and those who've robbed, or been robbed by, the larger economic system are being helped into productive work once again.

Will we seek and serve Christ in all persons, loving our neighbor as ourselves? We will, with God's help, for that is part of our share in God's mission.

Making Your Mark

Loving our neighbors means recognizing the body by the side of the road as a dignified human being, in need of mercy. What sorts of bodies are especially hard to recognize? Instead of just praying, "Lord have mercy," let your prayer be, "Lord let me be mercy; let us be mercy."

Spring Training

—⟋⟍m⟋—

There's a story about a head-to-head contest between Jesus and the devil. They were competing to see who could file away all the names in the book of life—on computer files. Each one had been working away madly for hours, when suddenly a flash of lightning blasted through the sky. Was the divine referee calling time? Maybe, but the devil lost. His computer crashed. "Jesus saves."

In our faith, in our scriptures, there's a recurring motif about the competition between the powers of self-concern and concern for God and others. Presumably, the devil lost because he was so focused on beating Jesus that he forgot to save his work. On the surface, that seems like a pretty innocent fault. Yet our understanding of sin is mostly about self-absorption. When we're so worried about ourselves that we can't think about others, there's something profoundly wrong.

That's what happens to Adam and Eve in the garden (Genesis 2–3). When the first human beings eat the fruit of the tree of knowledge of good and evil, their eyes are opened. The first consequence is realizing that they're naked, and it's not something they're terribly happy about. Unlike babies and little children who don't care, the first two human beings suddenly become modest, ashamed, and fearful. God strolls in the evening breeze looking for them, but they're hiding in the bushes. God calls out, "Where are you?" Their ability to delight in the presence of God has been compromised by their self-concern. Their attention has turned inward, away from their friendship with God.

The gospel reports of the temptations of Jesus are pretty similar (Matthew 4:1–11; Luke 4:1–13). After his long desert retreat, the devil challenges him to focus on filling his own needs. The devil sets those out as food, fame, and control. Adam and Eve were also after food, and control, and becoming like God. What they got was a pretty unsatisfying meal out of one piece of fruit, lives that felt *out* of control, and a sense of shame rather than acclaim.

Human beings continue to wrestle with self-centered and even selfish desire. But the life of faith invites us to look at how our loves are ordered. Where do we fix our hearts, and on what? Are we always thinking about ourselves? When we interact with others, are we mostly worried about how we are going to be treated, or what we're going to get?

Our fundamental problem as human beings is over-concern with self—what the church has for centuries called "original sin." We think about ourselves more than about our neighbors, rather than loving our neighbors *as* we love ourselves. If that balance is distorted, our relationship with God is equally distorted. Yet, by the grace of God, we have experiences that show us that the balance can be healthier—and holier—when we can get out of our own way. The selfless care of a parent for a small child, or the concern for a suffering mate or coworker, shows us something of what right love can look like. A little self-forgetfulness is a good thing, and it gets easier with practice.

The horror of the 2011 earthquake in Japan unleashed the experience of re-ordered loves, as people searched for the lost and cared selflessly for their injured and grieving neighbors. In life-or-death situations, many people can put aside an excessive self-concern. The challenge for most of us is to do a better job of it in daily life.

An essential part of our spiritual journey as Christians is about improving the balance between self-love and love of others. It's always a good time to practice—by remembering that the world is not all about *me*, whether that means sharing toys in the nursery or taking turns merging onto the highway, or figuring out that all we have is a gift, and it's meant to be shared. It's not easy—even Jesus wrestled with the lure of saying, "Me first." But there is abundant grace in the struggle.

Amazing things happen when we can let go of that obsession with our own selves and stuff. Not long ago, the congregation of St. David's Episcopal Church in East Greenbush, New York, gathered for a joy-filled dinner. That congregation is composed of many Burmese refugees, including long-settled, English-speaking homeowners as well as families who have just arrived from refugee camps. It also includes multigenerational New Yorkers and people from the West Indies. Members of St. David's and of other congregations help to support new immigrants with housing, clothing, employment, learning English, and discovering the nuances of living in the United States. A lot of potential divisions are being bridged in that joyous community. Together God's people are being served and blessed by that experience.

Not far away from St. David's, at the Capitol City Overflow Shelter in Albany, New York, men from the Gospel Rescue Mission are offered a nightly home through a ministry made possible by volunteers of faith from all over the city, and maybe the most amazing reality is that it's housed in a place that wasn't sure it wanted to welcome homeless people in the first place. St. Peter's Cathedral, and all the other Episcopal churches in the city, found a new life and possibility because they shifted their attention away from internal self-concern. Partners in Outreach was the result, and it's bringing new life and energy to the members of all of those churches, as well as blessing those who are being served and the volunteers who come to work. Transformation in the love of God abounds when self-focus and fear recede. That's what it looks like to put God's mission to serve others into practice.

But that takes spiritual discipline, like the training athletes undertake to run a better race, or play a more effective game. Jesus had his own spring training during his forty days in the desert. He resisted those temptations to satisfy cravings for instant fame or a tyrant's power, because he knew that they are poor substitutes for the blessing of friendship with God and neighbor.

The spiritual disciples of fasting, sharing resources or giving alms, prayer, and self-examination are all about recognizing that our self-centeredness won't bring the happiness we seek. Healing, health, and holiness come in finding the balance between loving neighbor, self, and God. There will be times when the journey feels more like Gethsemane than Eden, but the freedom to love rightly will bring us to resurrection, in company with the image of God all around us and within us. We might even rediscover the blessing of a walk in the evening breeze with a friend.

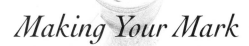

Making Your Mark

Where and how is self-concern getting in the way of serving neighbors?

PART IV

The Fourth Mark of Mission

To Seek to Transform Unjust Structures of Society

The Quest for Justice

The Abrahamic religions—Judaism, Christianity, and Islam—share a common framework for thinking about God. Though we don't share all the details, we do have a shared base for starting the conversation, and we can journey together for a very long way down that road. All three faith traditions talk about a restored world of peace and justice, where human beings live in right relationship with God and one another. The more familiar images or phrases for that vision are the reign of God, the peaceable kingdom, shalom, salaam. A number of them include a garden—both a reflection of the garden of Eden, from which human beings were expelled in the second creation story in Genesis, and the *pairidaeza* or walled garden, from which we get the word "paradise." The garden is about abundant food, good wine, and sacred relationships. All of these are highly particular visions of enough to eat and drink—and not mere adequacy, but the abundance for a feast. Human beings in this vision are living out their full lives, unafflicted by disease or sickness or war. That takes justice, where scarcity is unknown because resources are shared, and each lives rightly with others. All of this dream or vision is related to living in right relationship with God—or as some might put it, with the cosmos, with all that is.

Some of the bolder versions of this dream, like the one we find in the Hebrew Scripture in the Song of Songs, or in the poetry of some of the mystics in each tradition, move into a vision of holy and intimate union that is either the best of human sexual experience or human union with the Divine—or both.

The Abrahamic traditions offer this vision as the goal of human existence, even though various fundamentalizing tendencies in each tradition have pushed it out of this life into an afterlife, or insisted that the dream is only open to a privileged few who fulfill the fine points of religious law. At the core of each, however, is a parallel move from legalism toward compassion. The movement from law to compassion pervades the core, and compassion becomes the new understanding of moral good. Perception of beauty shifts as well, toward the innate beauty of creation. It's related to what I mentioned earlier about Irenaeus's quote regarding human liveliness: "The glory of God is a human being fully alive." That movement toward compassion also parallels the postmodernist movement from despair to aesthetics.

If compassion is essential to approaching God, what stands in the way? The ancient understanding is that our largest human failing is to think we are gods. The Abrahamic traditions understand that we reflect God, being made in God's image, that on a journey toward God we may even be on the road to becoming divine, but we are not God in fullness. Our self-focus stands in the way of our search for God, and in some sense always will, that being the way of things. But the cure is to turn outward, in compassion, toward those who are suffering. Righting human relationships is one avenue—the work of justice between human beings and in society—and relationships with all that are incrementally healed as a result. My relationship with God is healed as I ensure not only that my hungry neighbor is fed today, but as I work to prevent his future hunger. "Love God and love your neighbor as you love yourself" is the prime directive of faith. The way of compassion also means power is employed to change what is broken, unjust, suffering, or life-denying. Positive regard for those who differ is part of this work, and that reality is reflected in current research on the meaning of values. When societies move out of survival mode (where care and concern is usually reserved for one's closest relatives) into an economy[1] where knowledge is shared, that wide availability of knowledge itself makes it more possible to know and care for those who were formerly strangers, as personal anxiety about scarcity decreases.

But in addition to mere knowledge as a resource empowering transformation, the ability of empathy and compassion to change the world should compel our concern. Compassion is a vastly different kind of power—it grows in being shared and changes human hearts and societies in ways that the power of arms or domination cannot. This is the power made perfect in weakness of which Paul of Tarsus speaks (2 Corinthians 12:9); this power of compassion is effective by *not* invoking physical force. This is Gandhi's *satyagraha* or "soul-force," which informed Martin Luther King Jr.'s practice of nonviolence. This is the witness of Jonathan Myrick Daniels, who in the midst of the civil rights struggle in the early 1960s stepped in front of a fourteen-year-old African-American girl threatened by a racist's gun, and died for his trouble. This is the response to Matthew Shepard's death, and Tyler Clementi's, which are transforming attitudes toward gay and lesbian people. Whenever the life-denying impulses around us are met with an affirmation that life will only be more abundant in the absence of violence, transformation begins again.

The creative riposte to nihilism in favor of compassion for others sometimes takes remarkable forms. Connie Duckworth started Arzu to import handmade rugs from Afghanistan and wrote contracts with women weavers that bear up to a 50 percent bonus if they promise to send all their children, both daughters and sons, to school full-time, and if the household agrees to let the women attend literacy classes. In spite of the attempts of traditional norms to shut girls away from education, change is happening. Whatever the complexities around Greg Mortenson's *Three Cups of Tea*, the schools he has founded in Pakistan and Afghanistan are also changing reality. The recent spring of expectation in North Africa and the Middle East will never be put back in *purdah*—women will not be shut away forever; and the young women who've been arrested for having the temerity to drive in Saudi Arabia will not be forgotten.

The fact that the developed nations of the world collaborated in 2000, committing to reducing the worst of the world's poverty by half by the year 2015, has changed global reality. We are not likely to meet all the benchmarks of the Millenium Development Goals in the allotted time, but the possibility of a world that looks more like that ancient dream of plenty, justice, and peace will not likely be pushed back into an afterlife. People around the world will continue to hold that dream in their hearts. The power to move toward a beautiful, good, and true future for all humanity rests with us, and any who share the quest for God. We have a part in our neighbors' well-being. The death or mistreatment of any diminishes each of us, and we shall only know life more abundant when all begin to taste the feast.

In the Christian tradition, this amounts to saying that God lies in the direction of the way, the truth, and the life. The quest for God actually leads us toward the suffering of this world as we transform the unjust structures that account for their suffering. Only on that road will we discover the true, the beautiful, and the good.

Making Your Mark

Where is compassion moving in your life? What injustice is challenging you to act?

Turning the Tables

My husband and I went backpacking in northern Nevada one recent summer. We hiked up a trail that started at 8,500 feet, and then left it and climbed over a ridge well above 10,000 feet. We sat out a hail and thunderstorm on top of the ridge, then climbed down the other side to make a camp by a creek, still above 10,000 feet. We had rocks under our inflatable sleeping pads, and jackets for pillows instead of stones, and our dreams and midnight reflections were vivid. You simply can't see stars like that except at altitude, out in the middle of nowhere. It seemed like the doorway to heaven—and the wonder of stars, flowers, and the lakes and remnants of glacial scouring gave abundant evidence of their creator. I have a sense of what Jacob saw that night he spent in the wilderness (Genesis 28). And while he was afraid at the near presence of God, my own discomfort had to do with a strange breathing syndrome that happens to lots of healthy people at high altitude.[1] You wake up with the realization that you've stopped breathing, and then have a desperate urge to take a bunch of really deep breaths. It's very hard to go back to sleep, because the pattern continues, but there's really nothing wrong with you—you just keep feeling like you're going to die!

Experiences like that are often a gateway, an opening to an encounter with what is most real. Jacob's night in the wilderness gave him a taste of his connection to the source of all blessing, and he got a promise of land and descendants, and God's abiding presence with him, whatever road he took.

Where have our faith communities slept on a rock, or met God in the wild darkness? How have the families of the earth been blessed in us? Some may point to the growth of congregations and the number of people who show up for worship on Sunday morning, but blessing is not only about numbers. There is also blessing in those moments when we feel short of breath and aren't quite sure we can get enough oxygen to make it thirty more seconds. Most communities of faith have experienced that kind of desperation, and that sort of wakeful night.

Our sending is to be a blessing to others, but what will the blessing look like? We can't depend on evangelism by reproduction anymore—the postwar baby boom is long behind us. The growing parts of the church are overseas and in immigrant congregations, and they are also in those well-established congregations who examine the land and peoples around them and reach out to bless others and seek justice. I have met countless congregations who are clearly working at that, through initiatives that offer food, shelter, and basic needs. They are building Habitat homes, and feeding people, moving out into the community and wider world, seeking to bless those outside their walls.

Jacob went on the road, and Jesus went on the road. The psalmist says that both are blessed—those who dwell in the Lord's house and those who take the pilgrim's way. We come to church, and join faith communities, to be fed and equipped to go back out there and do God's work. We are people of the journey, even when it takes us into the wilderness. We cannot stay here.

Jesus's violent demonstration in the Temple (Matthew 21:12–17) was reserved for folks who thought they never had to go, who simply set up shop and stayed in the comfortable place—and then squeezed and exploited those who came in looking to meet God. I'd liken the experience of those Temple visitors to having somebody sit on your chest when you're struggling to breathe. Today's equivalent of those temple vendors might be the acquisitive preachers of a prosperity Ponzi scheme gospel, who say, "Give me your money and I will call down God's blessing on you." No, the real gospel of blessing is about prosperity for *all* people, it's about making sure that nobody goes hungry or lives in want.

Churches generally do a pretty good job of feeding the hungry people who show up on their doorsteps. We don't always do a very good job of going out to look for the hungry people in our communities, or asking why they're hungry in the first place. How many school kids in your neighborhood show up for class without breakfast? How many elders are shut in their homes without enough to eat or the ability keep themselves warm? Some of the worst hunger in this country is in the food deserts of inner cities and on Native American reservations. Are we seeing and meeting those hungry children of God? Will they be blessed through us? Will we be blessed through them?

People have been sitting in the temples of Wall Street, criticizing the buyers and sellers and trying to turn the tables, in a protest originally called Occupy Wall Street that has now expanded to cities around the world. It is fundamentally a protest against the concentration of wealth in fewer and fewer hands, and the ability of that wealth to control national and global political and economic realities. The basic critique is much like what Jesus was railing against in the Jerusalem Temple—some are getting rich by exploiting others. Making that comparison is making some people feel very short of breath. Yet what sort of blessing will we be? Jesus is present in the streets of New York City and Seattle and around the world, and he's asking why some are comfortable and others are hurting.

What kind of house is your church or faith community if it isn't in the business of setting all God's people free? Jesus's pilgrim way leads us out of the sanctuary and into a world in desperate need of more oxygen, and more of the basic stuff of life. Yes, we need to feed people when they're hungry, and we also need to ask why some are hungry when there is great abundance next door. And sometimes the tables need to be turned over. When Jesus did it, the coins sitting on those tables would have rolled out into the crowds, where people could pick them up. We can probably find better ways of seeing that the poor and hungry are fed. Can we do it without making them beg for the coins on the table? The ultimate goal is a table of abundance for all—God's table is set for all God's people, and the invitation has been sent out. Turn in here, and feast at the banquet prepared for you from the beginning of the world. We're the table waiters of that feast—and the cooks, finders of chairs, collectors of vegetables and cakes, rich wines and stew pots.

Who's hungry? Why? What can we do about it, and where and how will we share in setting the feast? That is part of our role in God's mission.

Making Your Mark

What are you doing to transform injustice in your neighborhood? Your city, state, and nation? What connection do you make with the reign of God?

Building Justice

In 1884, a group of West Indian sailors came ashore on Galveston Island, Texas. One of the first things they looked for was a church where people of African descent would be welcomed. Their spiritual quest led them to form the community of faith known as St. Augustine of Hippo, the oldest African American Episcopal church in Texas. Parishioners who worship there today may not know the names of any of those sailors who became their spiritual ancestors. They may not know anything else of the history of their founders, but they are still their heirs.

Each one of those sailors could have been called Isaiah, with a mouth like a sharp sword, hidden in the shadow of God's hand (Isaiah 49:1–6). Each was a polished arrow, hidden in the Lord's quiver. When the time came, when they had all tired of being shunted aside and told they weren't welcome in the Lord's house on the Lord's day, they went off to share words with Bishop Gregg, who answered their challenge. St. Augustine of Hippo was born, knit together in the crucible of struggle for justice, dignity, and equality.

Like Isaiah, we, too, are servants formed for God's prophetic work. We may labor faithfully, but become frustrated by the lack of progress. In our frustration, though, the prophet Isaiah continues to say to us, "I have labored in vain, I have spent my strength for nothing and for vanity." And what does God do but expand the task? Those who labor for justice on behalf of their own people often discover that their cause is the healing and salvation of all humanity.

Isaiah labored in the eighth century BCE, on behalf of the Hebrews, a divided and besieged, enslaved and hopeless people. His words of courage and strength bore an amazing challenge: "You will be light to the nations, to the whole world, not just your own people. Your salvation lies in being the healer of the nations" (Isaiah 49:6, my translation).

That message is as urgent today as it was more than 2,500 years ago. The sword and the arrow of God's word continue to pierce unyielding hearts and unjust societies. Consider Martin Luther King Jr., the servant who began his labors on behalf of the descendants of American slaves, in the same cause of justice that produced the church of St. Augustine of Hippo. He labored so that former slaves might be truly free, that his people might be able to eat and sleep and marry and work wherever they wished. And his cause expanded. His dream speech hints at it: the dream that his own children might be able to play together with all other children, and that when they were grown they might live in a nation that valued all for their virtues rather than their color. But he kept moving, particularly after the dark night experience in his kitchen that he called his mountaintop—it was his own "fear not, for you have seen the Lord" encounter, experienced by prophets before and after him, which impelled him to go out and do his work for justice. He became far more vocal and insistent that our work is peace, not war. He climbed that mountain and kept on shining, and his light has continued to shine in spite of the efforts of some to put it out. The light of the nations has shined in the darkness, and the darkness does not overcome it.

The church of St. Augustine of Hippo is a light shining in the darkness too, and its light grows stronger as members come to understand God's mission more widely. They are transforming unjust structures in society by feeding the hungry, teaching and healing the sick, feeding those who are hungry in body as well as soul through their garden, literally feeding the hungry volunteers who labor to rebuild Galveston after the devastation of hurricanes. Their urgent desire to serve new communities brings light to people from nations south of our border as well.

Perhaps the most revolutionary justice work that community does is through its art. The Bible isn't often seen as an art book, even though it's prompted a significant fraction of all the art that's been produced in the last two millennia. Visual arts are a remarkable way of reflecting the image of God, both in the creativity of the people who paint or draw, sculpt or photograph, and in the work they produce. The same can be said of musicians, dancers, and actors. The creator of the art shares God's own creativity in bringing that new work to light. The urge to create something beautiful or expressive reflects a desire to share in the divine, the transcendent, the holy. The creative act shares in God's own creativity, and it leads us beyond ourselves when it's shared.

Encouraging creativity gives people dignity by supporting those acts of co-creation. It can also foster reconciliation, for it invites us all to see the world in new ways. There is something profoundly creative about Jesus's own ministry of reconciliation, drawing unlikely people together to be fed in body and spirit.

The ability to create is vital to healing. Following the 2010 earthquake, the people of Haiti are still struggling to recover their sphere for creativity. Creativity follows very soon after food, water, and shelter in the list of human needs. The Episcopal cathedral in Haiti was famous—not just among Haitians—for the ways it fed the heart as well as the soul. It sheltered the major cultural institutions—the only music school and philharmonic orchestra in the country. Its children's choir, *Les Petits Chanteurs*—the Little Singers—has inspired people around the world through its tours. Both the choir and the orchestra are practicing in an open-air area behind the rubble of the cathedral, and they are already bringing comfort and hope to their neighbors across the nation. But it's probably the murals in the cathedral that are most known across the world.

They were painted in the early 1950s by native Haitian artists, in a naïf style that showed the great biblical stories happening in Haiti. Jesus is a Haitian, and so are the disciples. The women are Haitian market women, and you might see the children of the choir along the riverbanks in the baptismal mural. That's one of the three remaining murals which the Smithsonian has worked to conserve. Haitian Bishop Jean Zaché Duracin has insisted that the cathedral complex has to be the first priority for reconstruction, because it's going to feed the soul of the nation through the arts, through its schools—primary, secondary, music, and vocational—and through the ministry of the Sisters of St. Margaret.

The ability of Haitians to speak truth through the particular beauty of their own culture will be the peace- and justice-building sword and arrow. The art that emerges will help to heal not only Haiti, but the divisions between our own two nations, for there is much in our common history for which the United States needs to repent. The prophets who emerge in that place will serve a larger mission of justice, healing, and salvation.

When John the Baptist proclaims, "Here is the Lamb of God" (John 1:29), what comes to your mind? John's disciples have to recognize Jesus before they can follow. Those very words, "Lamb of God," only make sense in a particular context—today we only know what they mean because they've been explained over and over, often in pictures. John says that he recognized Jesus because he saw the spirit descend on him. What picture do you have of that? Jesus himself invites the disciples to "come and see." There is a whole lot of seeing and recognizing going on—and it continues here when you say to the world, "come and see" (John 1:39). Today we can come and see Jesus in the hope that's given in new murals at places like the church of St. Augustine of Hippo, and, in the creative work of carving dead tree stumps in Galveston. We can come and see God at work in the restoration and resurrection of Galveston, and in the art and music and dance in the rubble of the cathedral in Port-au-Prince. Come and see the love of God right here, gathering and feeding and healing.

Through our justice-building work, through actions and art, we can be light to the nations, telling the world to come and see.

Making Your Mark

Where has creativity helped to heal in your life?

Border Crossings

―――ᗰ―――

Whan Christians gather, we're meant to be an image of Jesus's dinner table, with all the nations drawn to the light of Christ—wherever we happen to be.

We gather as foreigners and as native dwellers in the land that God has created, to give thanks. That's the task of all of Jesus's followers—to say thank you for the healing that God offers us continually. We are to offer peace and hospitality in a community that extends that healing grace to others—to elders, to the hungry, to women and children seeking shelter from violence. That's the kind of healing Jesus gave the lepers—generous, whole-hearted, and unconcerned about the boundaries he was crossing and the expectations he was turning upside down.

In the gospel story about Jesus and the lepers, Jesus is doing something very surprising (Luke 17:11–19). As he travels through the region between Samaria and Galilee, he's crossing the social, political, and religious borders that kept Jews separate from Samaritans. *Those people*—and it was said that way in his day, too—were looked on as half-breed heretics, unfit for polite society. Good Jews just didn't interact with them. As a people, Samaritans were the offspring of intermarriage between the Jews who remained in Israel during the Babylonian exile and the occupiers of that nation—they were the mestizos of their day, rejected for being a mixed-race people. Their religion was also suspect, for they didn't worship in the Temple in Jerusalem like other Jews. Crossing over into Samaria,

Jesus puts himself in the midst of questionable people—foreigners, black sheep, oddball cousins. And when he heals the lepers, he sends them home so their healing can be certified—only their own kind can tell if the medicine "took."

Because of their visible skin disease, lepers, like Samaritans, were also kept outside polite society. Purity rules meant that others shouldn't come near a leper. They lived outside the city, shunned by others, and they had to announce their presence by calling out "unclean, unclean" whenever they approached others. The leper in the gospel story who turns back to say "thank you" to Jesus is also crossing a border that normally keeps well-defined groups separated. The one who comes back is a Samaritan *and* a leper—he's as much *other*, and therefore dangerous, as somebody in Jesus's day could imagine.

Border-crossing is intrinsic to all of Jesus's ministry. He's the icon and spokesperson for migration—as the Divine crosses the border between heaven and earth. The Apostles' Creed says he even goes as far as hell, which has until now been a place God doesn't visit. Hell is a place where people avoid God, refusing awareness of God or relationship with God—it's essentially a refusal of God. The Orthodox say that Jesus went into hell between Good Friday and Easter in search of the lost—Adam, Eve, and Judas, among others. There's a wonderful icon that shows Jesus literally dragging Adam and Eve out of hell by their wrists.

In healing the leper, Jesus, the divine boundary-crosser, leaps over the chasm between clean and unclean. He does it again in greeting the Samaritan. And he continues to invite us to join him, crossing boundaries and healing division. That's about right relationships, or *justice*.

And that is what the Body of Christ is most fundamentally about. It is a place where national and ethnic boundaries no longer divide. We are to be a people of radical thanks-giving, a community that includes those who are often excluded—the old and forgotten, the

abused and ashamed, and all of God's creatures who have been separated in some way or other from the banquet God intends for us all.

The words of the prophet Jeremiah still ring true today, some
2,600 years later:

> "These are the words of the letter that Jeremiah sent
> from Jerusalem to the remaining elders among the
> exiles, and to the priests, the prophets, and all the peo-
> ple, whom Nebuchadnezzar had taken into exile from
> Jerusalem to Babylon.... Thus says the Lord of hosts,
> the God of Israel, to all the exiles whom I have sent
> into exile from Jerusalem to Babylon: Build houses and
> live in them; plant gardens and eat what they produce.
> Take wives and have sons and daughters; take wives for
> your sons, and give your daughters in marriage, that
> they may bear sons and daughters; multiply there, and
> do not decrease. But seek the welfare of the city where
> I have sent you into exile, and pray to the Lord on its
> behalf, for in its welfare you will find your welfare."
>
> (29:1, 4–7)

You may not be in Eden again, Jeremiah tells his listeners, or in the
home you knew in Jerusalem. But build homes anyway, he insists.
Plant gardens and harvest them, raise children and seek the welfare
of the city where you are, for in its welfare you will find your own.

That is the story of the migrant. Increasingly, no city in this
world would exist without the willingness of people to move from
one place to another and build a home in a strange land. Our communities will thrive as long as residents and newcomers cooperate
in building a healed, just society, a better community for all people.
We do it most essentially by working together—planting gardens,
educating children, healing the suffering around us, and dreaming
dreams of welcome and peace.

The ability to do that hard work comes from gratitude. The ability to give thanks at a deep level comes from realizing that we didn't really achieve those blessings all on our own. Somebody helped, gifts were given, God had a part in this. What can we do but turn around and say, "thank you"? What are we grateful for? What healing have we received?

Not long ago I met several boundary crossers—three groups of people giving thanks and offering healing at the same time—all of them from St. James's Episcopal Church in Milwaukee, Wisconsin. One group told me about burial services for the poor—people with no relatives to claim their bodies or put them to rest among friends. These burials are paid for by the county, because there is literally no one else to do it. A small contingent of people from that parish attend the burial, offering prayers and flowers, and stand watch at the grave as mortal remains are committed to the earth. These burial ministers become family to strangers.

I also learned about a group in the parish who sort clothes for Red Door, which provides access to clothing two Saturdays a month. They meet their guests with dignity, assist them in finding clothes that fit, and ensure that there are enough clothes for all.

Finally, I met with the coordinators of The Gathering, a feeding ministry that serves breakfast five days a week, as well as a Saturday lunch. They receive a couple of hundred hungry people each time, in dignity and as honored guests. One of the leaders has been working there for over twenty-eight years. Those tables become family dinner tables.

Each of these ministries is about boundary crossing, as the living meet the dead, and the adequately clothed, fed, and housed meet the hungry and homeless. All the workers I met talked about how they receive so much more from their guests and clients than they offer. They are all deeply grateful for the privilege of being able to serve. That gratitude overflows into greater service (ministry), and community is built in spite of the boundaries, borders, and blocks that arise when we see some people as *other*.

Maybe the most essential gift is to understand ourselves as foreigners and strangers, for none of us yet lives in the wholly healed world for which we were made. We haven't yet reached that home. Yet if we do as Jeremiah urges and build houses and live in them, plant gardens and eat their produce, shape and nurture all sorts of families, the welfare of the cities where we find ourselves does begin to move toward the heavenly city we're all still searching for. The work of Christians is to keep migrating, keep crossing the boundaries, for then we will indeed begin to find our way home.

Making Your Mark

What borders have you crossed in seeking justice in your community? How has gratitude motivated you?

Minding the Gap

Three blocks from The Episcopal Church Center in New York is a public park called Dag Hammarskjöld Plaza. It's the site of many rallies, a weekly farmers' market, and the occasional protest, since it's across the street from the United Nations. I visited this park before dawn once, and ran by what I thought was a person standing alone. I quickly met others, sitting on benches or standing around. These weren't living people, but a new sculpture installation—twenty-six human forms lined up through the block-long plaza. They were life-sized statues, half of them of cast iron, and half of cast aluminum. There were thirteen pairs, in different attitudes, an iron figure mirroring the stance of an aluminum one—sitting, standing, puzzled, welcoming, even one pair bent over on their knees in prayerful contemplation. Twelve pairs lined up, and a thirteenth pair embracing all the others—with one at each end of the park. The figures were cast by an Icelandic artist, Steinunn Thorarinsdóttir, who calls the installation *Borders*.

This collection of human forms has haunted me. White and black, black and white, engaged in the same acts of life, reaching out for relationship—each member of these pairs faces the other. They are not living in parallel, ignoring each other, nor are they turned away, or going apart. Yet there is still a space needing to be crossed between them—the ones closest together are the ones in prayer, and they're still a good ten feet apart. These are like the ones the Apostle Paul speaks of—those who are near and those who are far off (Ephesians 2:13–17). The borders have something to do with their different colors—a rich, rusty brown, or a matte silver-gray—and with the space between them.

In our history those borders have been implemented as a value judgment and used to condone all sorts of injustice. Yet the color line hasn't always been the only source of inhuman behavior—white Americans have turned other immigrants like the Irish and the Italians into wage slaves, and Africans were deeply involved in enslaving fellow Africans. Other color lines have been used to excuse vast indignities committed on Native Americans and Asian Americans and today's grievous inhumanity to Latino migrants in our midst. Those kinds of borders have too often become bonds of injustice, yokes of oppression, and the finger pointing and evil speech that the prophet Isaiah condemns (Isaiah 58:6–12).

Human beings are capable of the most wretched behavior—as the confession in the old Book of Common Prayer put it, "There is no health in us." Yet through human prophets God continues to call us to turn in a new direction, toward healing, wholeness, and holiness of life. In the wider world, we call that justice. Some have said that justice is simply love in public action. Justice is what Isaiah is talking about when he tells his listeners to feed the hungry, house the homeless, cover the naked, emancipate the slaves, and redeem prisoners. Jesus reads from the same prophet when he claims anointing to bring good news to the poor, sight to the blind, freedom to slaves and prisoners, and to proclaim the year of God's favor (Luke 4:16–19).

We know something about the consequences of having "no health in us." Many faith communities work to turn away from the prison pipeline, and the multi-generational consequences of poverty, and the great gaps between current reality and our national aspirations for life, liberty, and the pursuit of happiness—for all God's children. There is an enormous breach in that promise. We have not yet found the year of the Lord's favor.

When Isaiah urges us to turn toward a society of justice, he promises that those who set the captives free, feed the hungry, and stop the finger pointing and hate speech will be called repairers of the breach, and restorers of streets to live in. We're all hungry for those safe and healthy cities, where we can grow old watching children play in those streets, growing into health and abundant life in a community of peace. That is the ancient dream of God's people. It is the promised land, Zion, and the beautiful city of God. It may be a long way down the road, but we move a few steps closer to it with each step toward justice and reconciliation.

How are we going to close that breach, and restore those streets, and build that city? Paul offers a hint—reminding us that Jesus has already broken down the walls between us: the borders of color and race and gender and language (Ephesians 2:13–22; Galatians 3:28). We are all children of the same God, we're all searching for that same city of abundant life. We do not have to remain strangers to each other, for we are citizens of the same, heavenly realm, fellow travelers on the same Jesus road.

What maintains those borders? What keeps us twenty feet apart, wary of those who don't look like us, or speak with a different accent? Whomever we call *other* is the image of God, and none of us will be complete until we can embrace another aspect of God's good creation. Without moving toward the *other*, the breach continues. The fear that keeps us on edge and distant never leads to healing. Why is it that the angels always start their announcements by saying, "Fear not"? Encountering the image of God is usually challenging, but it's not eternally deadly—death and diminishment and despair come from avoiding the image of God. We should be praying for courage to cross the space between us. That's where the journey to freedom begins—in reaching out to the image of God so close at hand, without whom we will never be free or whole.

There's a poem that's famous among aviators, written by a young pilot in the Second World War. He was the son of an Episcopal priest who had crossed other boundaries to serve as a missionary in China. Most people think the poem is about the glory of flying. It is. Yet I think it's even more deeply about the courage to keep reaching out across whatever separates us from God. Think of being sent like an angel to a neighbor, bearing the message, "Fear not." The first and last lines of the poem are:

> Oh, I have slipped the surly bonds of earth …
> put out my hand and touched the face of God.[1]

I share a love of that poem with an African American pilot, now well into his eighties, who flew more than a hundred missions in Vietnam. He loves flying so much that he learned to maintain airplanes, too. He's still flying, and still doing aircraft maintenance and inspections. I give thanks for his gifts, and for the gruff and gentle way he's challenged me to grow—both as a pilot and a pastor. He's shown me something of the face of God.

Touching the face of God is our work, of whatever mettle/metal our craft may be—iron or aluminum, or some new and holy alloy— it can and must bear us Godward, to bridge the borders between us. Fear not. Courage will bear us across.

Making Your Mark

What gaps are apparent in your community? Where do you need courage to reach across?

Living the Dream

In the calendar of The Episcopal Church, we mark the feast of William Wilberforce on July 30. We remember this member of Parliament for his forty-year struggle to end slavery in the British Empire, which finally succeeded in 1833. In the United States it took another thirty years, and it was another sixty years before the slave trade finally ended in Zanzibar. Yet even today there are slaves in many places across the globe. Children are sold into slave labor in Asia; girls, women, and boys are forced into slavery to serve profit motives and sexual desires; and people are enslaved in Africa as laborers or soldiers. Some children still work as "fish slaves" in the lakes of the Great Rift Valley of East Africa.

There are other kinds of slavery than physical bondage. The poverty or hopelessness in which some people live is a virtual kind of slavery, which makes a mockery of the kind of abundant life for which we were created.

Those who join the work of Jesus, especially his insistence that he came to bring abundant life, are linked to the anti-slavery crusade of William Wilberforce, to the work of Desmond Tutu and Martin Luther King Jr. for ending racial segregation, to the work of Mother Teresa of Calcutta in caring for the forgotten, and the labors of saints through the ages. Christians know that as part of Christ's body they are made for freedom and abundant life. Jesus tells his disciples that he came that we might have life, and have it abundantly. Our work as part of his body is to help make that abundant life a reality for others. That's what justice is ultimately about.

The Apostle Paul tells us in his letter to the Galatians: Because we have joined the family of Jesus Christ, we have left slavery and become heirs of the promises made to Abraham and our ancestors (Galatians 3:26–29). Together with all other members of God's family, we have become heirs of the "year of the Lord's favor" (Luke 4:19). That's an ancient way of talking about the reign of God—a society in which the poor receive good news, the sick are healed, the hungry fed, and slaves and prisoners are set free. It is shalom; it is peace with justice.

The promises made in Christian initiation are about continuing that abundant life work. We promise to bring good news to the poor, heal the blind, set the captives free, and proclaim good news about the coming kingdom—because we believe that all God's children are meant to have abundant life. Each of us plays a part in that work.

Abundant life work is often called "mission" in the church—it's what we're sent to do as the Body of Christ. It's what Christians promise to do in the world as followers of Jesus. Some people think mission is only about evangelism, and they quote the part of Matthew that says, "Go, baptize, and make disciples of all nations" (Matthew 28:19, my summary). Others cite another part of Matthew that says the kingdom of heaven belongs to those who care for the least of these (Matthew 25:31–46). They are both essential—we cannot love God and love our neighbors as ourselves unless we are doing both.

When I visited the Congo, Zambia, and Botswana, everywhere I turned, I saw Christians turning outward, to share the good news they know in Jesus with others who need hope and healing. They are working with victims of sexual violence, with orphans, with those who have HIV. In each place they are showing and teaching about the love of God in Jesus as they meet people in need.

As Christians, we say "yes" to joining this mission, and this is what we are sent out to do. What is your part in God's mission going to look like—in congregation, city, nation—and in the wider world?

How will we proclaim good news, given the bad news in the world around us? What part of God's dream for a healed world most needs to be heard?

We start with holding up that dream. God didn't create us to live in conditions of war or violence, God created us and set us in a garden where no one was hungry. We're not meant to be sick or have no access to healing. We start proclaiming good news by naming the dream and how that differs from current reality. And then we start on the work of changing what is into what is meant to be. It's not easy, but it starts with the dream and the insistence that as God's children, loving our neighbors means working to change that current reality, and beginning to move toward the dream.

Consider what Jesus says after he reads from that vision of Isaiah's: "Today this scripture has been fulfilled in your hearing" (Luke 4:21). That is a highly appropriate and significant charge for all Christians, indeed for all people of faith. Each of us is an essential part of making that dream reality. Where will we spend ourselves? To what will we commit the gifts God has given us? How will we begin to understand the things that bring us joy as gifts for the mission God has given us?

Whatever our gifts—sports, cooking, mathematics, leadership— God can use them. If we will offer our gift, God will use it. May the gifts we present to God be offered for more abundant life, and a healed world—that vision of justice and peace.

Making Your Mark

What part of God's dream for a healed world most needs to be heard in your own context? Where do your own gifts connect?

Enough for Everyone

Not long ago, I spent nearly two weeks traveling in Africa. With my fellow travelers, we received immense hospitality everywhere we went. At every stop, we were offered food and drink and fellowship and welcomed with song, prayer, worship, and great rounds of hand-shaking. We were fed even on very short journeys when we expected to receive nothing. Strangers welcomed us with open arms, and we discovered new friends. It was a continuing reminder that hospitality, friendship, and peace begin in satisfying human hungers. We encountered abundance everywhere, even in the midst of what the world calls poverty.

The prophet Isaiah (55:1–5) talks about the desire to fill what is empty. He speaks the words of Wisdom, urging God's people to seek only what will ultimately satisfy. The psalmist reminds us that God is full—of compassion, kindness, righteousness, mercy, and is indeed the source of all the abundance we can know or imagine (Psalm 145:8–22). Jesus, in the ultimate example of living in a spirit of abundance, feeds the multitude from a few loaves and fishes (Matthew 14:13–21).

In Matthew's gospel, Jesus, having just heard of the death of John the Baptist, is trying to find some time and space in which to grieve. King Herod has murdered his cousin and friend, and now Jesus must carry on, but he's going to grieve first. Yet the people who have followed him all through Galilee won't leave him alone. These people are hungry for God's wisdom, and they know that Jesus has something that satisfies. They've followed him along the shore even while he's out in the middle of the lake.

When Jesus comes ashore, he responds to their hungers with compassion, and he offers healing. As the dinner hour approaches, the disciples want him to send the people off to the local towns to find some food. But Jesus won't ignore their hunger, and he won't let the disciples off the hook. "You give them something to eat" (Matthew 14:16). Jesus invites them to answer the hunger themselves, but they respond out of scarcity. "We have nothing here," they say, "except these bits of bread and fish." But Jesus doesn't see scarcity; he sees abundance, and in the end, the gospel says, "all ate and were filled," and baskets of leftovers remained, even after thousands of people had eaten.

Here is Isaiah's dream of a great banquet on a hillside brought to reality. Here is a snapshot of the kingdom of God—people healed, fed, satisfied, picnicking on the grass in peace. It's an insistence that God has created us for a world where there is abundance, where no one is hungry. And it requires the disciples' participation, even when they can't see the abundance.

What are people hungry for? Food and water, yes, and desperately so in parts of the world, especially in Kenya, Somalia, and Ethiopia. Cholera has erupted along the Congo River because people can't find clean water. People have been desperately hungry for peace in Sudan for generations, and, in spite of ongoing international concern, there has been profound hope as South Sudan begins independence. Wherever I traveled in Africa, I met people eager to send children to school, making remarkable sacrifices to earn school fees, starting neighborhood schools for orphans, seeking partnerships to ensure that children can continue their schooling beyond what is immediately available. People everywhere are deeply hungry for justice and an end to violence. And everywhere in the world, people want to know they are loved, that they matter, that somehow their existence is more than hunger.

Jesus answers all those hungers. He reminds us that we are God's beloved, and that God is always concerned for us; he calls us "friend." Jesus feeds, he heals, he brings the good news of God's dream of a world of peace and justice. And he challenges his followers to join in building a world where those hungers are filled. "You give them something to eat," he says to us. "You feed their hunger."

The world is beginning to answer the starvation in Ethiopia and the horn of Africa. People are responding to the hungers in countless communities in that part of the world. God needs all of us to join in that work. Will we answer? We are disciples of Jesus, who says the same to us: "You give them something to eat." If we offer what we have, God will bless it. It will be enough, and there will be leftovers for those who haven't yet arrived. With God's blessing, all will be satisfied, if we will join the work of feeding our hungry sisters and brothers.

An Anglican bishop in Africa, Trevor Huddleston, wrote a well-known prayer for Africa: "God bless Africa. Guard her people, guide her leaders, and give her peace." That powerful and simple vision is God's, for the whole world: God's mission is to fill those who are hungry. Our task is to join in the feeding, that all may know peace.

Making Your Mark

How will you help fill the hunger for justice and peace?

Created for Life

The Exodus story is more than three thousand years old, but it expresses fears that are very modern. The Egyptians, relying on the Hebrews as foreign labor, are afraid in the same way many Americans are today. *Are the Jews out-populating us?* they wonder. Today some worry about Muslims, or Mormons, or Latino immigrants. We hear those fears being stirred on talk radio, about how all *"those people*, the ones who aren't the mainstream of what America is *really* all about, who are just here by sufferance, or here to work illegally—just look at them! They're having so many children that they're going to conquer us by force of numbers." More than a thousand years before the birth of Jesus, the Egyptians were worried about pretty much the same things that worry some today.

In the twenty-first-century United States, population pressure is mostly understood in economic terms: "All *those people*" are taking away jobs that belong to "real Americans." We usually ignore the realities that this nation has prospered largely because of the hard work and creativity of continuing waves of immigrants, people who value the possibilities of education and a better life here than what they knew at home.

The response to population growth in some parts of the world has been like Pharaoh's—limit the number of children that are produced. Starting in 1979, China said that most couples could only have one child, and in addition to a lower birth rate, it's produced a terrible warping of the gender balance. There will soon be millions

of young Chinese men who have no chance of finding a female partner. Something similar is happening in India, where far more boy
babies are born than girls. Pharaoh tried to eliminate the boy babies,
but modern societies are often eliminating the girls.

Others fear the increasing burden that the vast human population is placing on this planet—the garden is overpopulated, at least if
its members expect the kind of lifestyle that the first world enjoys. In
2011, *National Geographic* ran a yearlong series on population issues.
There was a fascinating article on the "anthropocene age"—the current geologic age, characterized most clearly by human impact. Our
heavy human footprint on this planet is impacting the ability of
other species to survive, and extinction rates are skyrocketing. The
human manipulation of our day may not be as conscious as Pharaoh's, but it has the very same potential for death.

What are we supposed to do with the fear and death all around
us? The September 11, 2001 attacks on the World Trade Center
happened over a decade ago, and we're still at war in places that
most Americans knew nothing about ten years ago. Our national
politics are a disgraceful game of "gotcha" or flat-out refusal to play.
We have lost the sense that together, we have the potential to build
a society far more life-giving than what we see around us. It's surprising to many that the Islamic nations of the Middle East and North
Africa have recently shown such hopeful responses, as their people
rise up against tyrannical and exploitative governments that haven't
served the good of the whole population.

The story of Moses and his sister Miriam and Pharaoh's daughter
(Exodus 1:8–2:10) is a reminder that supposed enemies, people of
different faiths, varied tribes, and both genders, are all necessary to
God's mission of a healed world. In Pharaoh's plan, Moses was supposed to be food for the Nile crocodiles, but his mother and sister
figured out a creative way to get him fostered by the royal family.
The compassion of Pharaoh's daughter eventually brought down her
own father's tyranny and set the Israelites free. She was able to look

beyond the divisions between immigrant (Israelite) laborers and the ruling Egyptian population and act in the same way that the Israelite midwives did—rejecting the death-dealing of Pharaoh. *No, she said, this child shall live!* There were many saviors of Israel—including the midwives, who disobeyed Pharaoh's order to kill the boys born to Israelite women, the mother and sister of Moses who crossed boundaries to ensure life for the boy, and Pharaoh's daughter, who took him in and raised him as her own.

Moses eventually became the route to greater life for his people. He was also a savior of his people. There is more than a passing resemblance between his name in Hebrew, *Moshe*, and what Peter calls Jesus, *Mashiah*, Messiah, son of the living God. Who is our God but the source of life, and life abundant?—and sender of Messiah, anointed and appointed to bring greater life for all God's people?

When Jesus asks his friends who people think he is, they identify several prophets, of whom Moses is the first in biblical history (Matthew 16:13–20). Prophets speak or act on behalf of God—they tell it like it is, or show what God's country ought to look like—and it is always about abundant life. You know the images—lion lying down with a lamb, an end to hunger and war, former enemies sitting down to a banquet together, no one dying young. It's a vision in which the injustice of the world has been transformed into something entirely different. Peter gets it, for once. "You are the Messiah," he responds to Jesus's question. He sees in Jesus a sign of God's presence, the one who will lead us to that kind of abundant life.

We all know that the journey toward abundant life is not easy. It got Jesus executed, and it got Peter executed, and it has gotten many other prophets executed. Yet the promise of abundant life still stands before us all. It's bigger than debates over deficits, and who is to blame for the economic mess we're in. It's bigger than narrow ethnic identities or me-first attitudes. That vision of abundant life is the road Jesus showed us, the same one Paul reminds us of in his letter to the Romans: Present yourselves as a living sacrifice, don't just go along with the ways of this world, but transform those ways into godly ones that lead to more abundant life (Romans 12:1–8). And remember that the gifts of every person are necessary and honorable—we need each other. All the members of God's creation have something to contribute to abundant life, and all will enjoy it when the whole body becomes a holy, life-giving body.

What might it mean to present our bodies as a living sacrifice? We often think of that word "sacrifice" as a limitation, or a giving up. It's more accurate to think of it as a making holy, a setting apart for a special purpose. Abundant life doesn't just mean more lives—it means the ability of all to live in peace, with adequate resources and an end to strife. It means creating a world in which society's injustices are addressed. How can we put our gifts to work and join God's creative work of abundant life?

Our world is facing enormous pressures, but there is something we can do about it. Maybe, like Pharaoh's daughter, we'll show compassion to a lost child—by teaching a little girl to read, or by being a big brother or sister to a boy who has none. Or maybe we'll help refugees or immigrants find a place in this society so that they, too, may find their life-giving vocation. Maybe our contribution to abundant life is about gardens and rain barrels and bike lanes and solar panels—to help all of us live more lightly on this earth so that all may simply live. Or perhaps we are working to build schools for girls in developing nations so there won't be so many child brides—and those girls can make their own choices about when and how many children they'll bear—and be better able to provide for them. Each is a way of transforming society and offering more abundant life—not just more lives lived in misery.

Those are the keys to the kingdom that Jesus was talking about. When we bind people together into a body that builds up others, we are helping to build abundant life in Jesus's name. When we loose people from old sins, when we forgive them, we are doing the same thing. Abundant life is not something that simply appears[1]—it is a creative work of the Body of Christ. It is a living sacrifice, and it needs the partnership of all of us, and the whole world, so that the whole world may finally know the abundant life for which God created every one of us and every part of creation.

Each of us can become a living sacrifice, so that more of the world may know the abundant life for which each one was created.

Making Your Mark

For what special purpose have we been set apart? What gifts do we bring to this journey toward abundant life?

Tending the Vine

Absalom Jones was the first black priest in The Episcopal Church, and when he died, he was still the only one. He was born in slavery in Delaware in 1746, became a house slave as a child, and was sent to Philadelphia at age sixteen to work in his master's store. He taught himself to read and write, met and married his wife, bought her freedom, and after several more years, by working together, they bought his freedom as well. He worshiped in a Methodist community while it was still part of the Anglican family, where white and black attended together. That is, until the black community began to grow, under his leadership and that of Richard Allen, another Methodist lay leader.

That growing black membership caused the white vestry to decree that they would have to worship in an upstairs gallery, and one Sunday morning the ushers tried to move them out of their pews. When the process changed from words to physical removal, the black community walked out. All this was going on while the words of the Declaration of Independence were still echoing in the world's ears, at the very moment when the first amendment and its guarantees of civil rights were being considered by the new states. It turned out that justice was for some, but not yet for all. Freedom of religion and freedom of association were guaranteed in that first amendment, but it has taken many years to move toward their reality for all, and we are not yet fully there.

Jones and Allen left St. George's Methodist Episcopal in 1786 and founded what was effectively a nondenominational congregation.

The Free African Society was a fellowship for mutual aid and support, not unlike the early Christian communities written about in the Book of Acts. In a deep echo of Jesus's words, "I no longer call you servants, but friends" (John 15:15, my translation), the Free African Society treated all members as friends, caring for widows and orphans, tending the sick, burying the dead, encouraging financial interdependence, and generally sharing each other's burdens and joys.

By 1794 the Methodists had separated from the Anglicans in the United States, and the congregation of friends voted on which denomination to join. Most chose to remain with the historic body now called The Episcopal Church. Richard Allen was among those who left, and he eventually founded the African Methodist Episcopal Church.

Jones's group approached the Episcopalians in Pennsylvania, seeking admission as St. Thomas African Episcopal Church, on the condition that they govern themselves as a separate parish, with the ability to call and support their own clergy. The diocesan convention agreed, and Absalom was called to ordination. The same convention made clear that they would not seat delegates from St. Thomas in their annual convention, a policy that was not reversed until the 1860s.

Bishop William White ordained Absalom Jones as a deacon in 1795. In a pattern of lengthy delay that would be repeated with others, Jones wasn't ordained a priest until 1802. Peter Williams was the next black man to be ordained a priest, in 1826. The first Native American was ordained eighty-six years after Absalom Jones, but David Pendleton Oakerhater remained a deacon for fifty years, at a time when there were almost no vocational deacons.

Despite attitudes in the church that tried to keep St. Thomas and other African American communities separate and unequal, Jones faithfully served St. Thomas and the wider community until his death in 1818, becoming known as the black bishop of The Episcopal Church.

The wounds of slavery, racial injustice, and division continue to this day, within the church and beyond it. Relationships between The Episcopal Church and the African Methodist Episcopal Church (AME) are still strained, in spite of many years of attempted healing. The body known as Churches Uniting in Christ includes the AME and The Episcopal Church, and two other historically black church bodies also derived from segregation, the Christian Methodist Episcopal Church (CME) and the African Methodist Episcopal Zion Church (AME Zion). Peter Williams was brought up in the AME Zion, but chose The Episcopal Church as the place to pursue ordained ministry. Efforts to build bridges and trust across these historic divisions have been tainted by racism, even though we share a great deal of history, tradition, and theology. The good news is that the whole of that body is committed to working on issues of racism.

Discovering and affirming our connections is one way of strengthening the vine. The branches can't stay connected to the vine without acknowledging other branches. As the same sap flows through that vine, the blood of Christ courses through all our veins. Division, oppression, racism, and all the ways in which we try to separate ourselves only deny the reality of our interconnection. None of us will be healed until all those connections are put back together, and truth and justice begin to restore trust.

Dialogue with the AME, AME Zion, and CME churches is beginning to lead toward common ministry. The near-term focus is how we might partner for rebuilding in Haiti, and we hope to educate our members about the history of relationships between Haiti and the United States, much of it with pretty wretched overtones of racism.

We will go on looking for ways to reconcile our understanding of ministry. At some point in the long years of dialogue, we apparently got stuck on the ministry of bishops. The clear sense has been given that we think our historic episcopate is better or fuller than theirs, and that coming together in full communion would require some recognition that theirs was deficient. Any liturgical celebration of that full communion would require that the Episcopal bishops lay hands on the Methodist Episcopal bishops to convey the fullness of the historic episcopate. I think it's fair to say that that was perceived as racism dressed up as theology.

Something fascinating happened recently in Pennsylvania. I was among a group that celebrated a full communion relationship between The Episcopal Church and the Moravian Church. That liturgy involved the mutual laying on of hands—first the Episcopal bishops knelt to have hands laid on by the Moravians, and then the roles were reversed. Perhaps we have learned something about diversity of gifts. Maybe it helped that there were black bishops and white bishops on both sides that night. The Episcopal Church must also recognize that we have gifts to receive from the Methodist Episcopal churches and amends to make for the scandal of separation over race.

That vine holds fast to the saints, and Absalom Jones, Richard Allen, Peter Williams, and David Pendleton Oakerhater are reconciled to each other in Jesus. Our part in God's mission is to work on the rest of the communion of saints—those of us still walking around.

How can we increase the connections among us in this life? By telling the stories, in all their grief and sin and joy, and trying once again to stop lopping off branches and heal the grafts which bind us all to the same vine.

For freedom Jesus has set us free—yet we will only be truly free when we acknowledge all those grafts and branches as abundant blessing.

Making Your Mark

What branches can you see that have been lopped off? How might you and those around you help grafts to grow and heal?

Casting Out Demons

—⟋m⟍—

Have you met any demons lately? As heirs of the apostles, we too, have received power over them—Jesus, after all, charged his followers to expel demons wherever they turned up—and the charge to heal disease and proclaim the reign of God is our charge as well (Luke 9:1–6). And as the Nike slogan says, we're supposed to "just do it" without any excuses or excess baggage.

There are demons aplenty, even if we don't recognize them as easily as our first-century counterparts did. Daniel Deng Bul, archbishop of Sudan, visited New York recently, warning of the demons that were about to be unleashed in his country. The long-promised referendum in Sudan's Comprehensive Peace Agreement took place in January 2011. The people of South Sudan had a date with destiny to decide whether to become a separate nation or to remain united with the north. In anticipation, the Khartoum government staged tanks and soldiers on the border with the South—and the border keeps moving farther south every time there's a new oil discovery. Archbishop Daniel and the other religious leaders with him spied the demons in Sudan, and they've told the world about them.

Three million Sudanese have died in the civil wars there. More are expected to die. The four horsemen are about to be unleashed again—Sudan knows them far too well, as conquest, war, famine, and death have been companions for years. The nations of the world, including the United States, have a duty to respond—and the power and authority to do so. The question is whether we have the will. Will we stand by and let Sudan become another Rwanda, or will we work for justice?

Yet even in the midst of the looming possession of a great swath of Sudan, many are working to heal, feed, and proclaim the good news of the reign of God. Doing so makes the demons easier to discern. And that may be the messianic secret—when the spirit within proclaims the reign of God, the demonic stands out so starkly that it's hard to miss.

Daniel told me that he has plans for four hospitals in Sudan. He inherited a debt of $300,000 when he became archbishop. In just a few years, he paid off all but $60,000, but that meant laying off almost all of the staff. He needs entrepreneurs, people who can find creative ways to build and heal the larger community, and equally creative ways to fund it. Schools are being built and operated to teach children and adults, and more are needed. The Episcopal Church of Sudan is indeed healing, feeding, and proclaiming good news, but it needs partners to advocate, pray, give and lend funds, and build. Above all else, the people of Sudan need peace if their work is to be fruitful, and peace is only possible when the injustice and division there are announced and dealt with.

Healing division and injustice is gospel work in all nations. The "common cathedral" in Boston is modeled directly on what Jesus was up to—healing, feeding, and proclaiming the good news of the kingdom to anybody who turned up. That is a ministry of justice, and it has begun to wander around the country, offering shalom in one city after another. That good news is lighting fires of hope in city squares, marketplaces, and under bridges from San Francisco to Seattle to Kansas City to New Haven. In the aftermath of the earthquake, Port-au-Prince now has an open-air cathedral as well—it is their proclamation of the indestructibility of the peaceable kingdom.

We were made for that reality of lions lying down with lambs, where human beings don't learn war any more. The demons of our inner cities and poverty-possessed communities scuttle around in grievous contrast. The ministry of schools like Epiphany School in Dorchester, Massachusetts, witnesses to the possibility of exorcising those demons and healing whole societies. The fifth through eighth grade students there may be the immediate focus, but their families are drawn into a new community as well, and the larger impact is immense. The sparks of hope within those children are like wildfire, setting off explosions of new possibility in each one they touch. Schools and teachers who invest in hope, whether in Massachusetts, Haiti, or Sudan, drive out demons of despair, dysfunction, and death.

The publication *Episcopal Life* shared an opinion piece a while back by a young Teach for America volunteer, Michael Drawbaugh. He was working in Allen, South Dakota, which at last count was the poorest community in the United States. It's 95 percent Lakota, and the median *family* income in 2000 was $3,800. Michael talks about his experience of confirmation, then challenges the rest of us:

> The call comes to you now; I do not think I am pre-
> pared to fight against injustice alone. What will you do,
> Baptized Christian, to eliminate educational inequality
> in your community and nation? What will you do to
> ensure that schools represent the freedom, equality,
> and acceptance which we have found in Christ's King-
> dom? How will you live out your Baptismal Covenant
> in a world that needs your attention? The need is great
> and the time is short.[1]

Michael has been well-schooled in the good news of the reign of God, he's recognized the power and authority he's been given, and the community in Allen has been the beneficiary. He has been cast-ing out demons—in blessing one child at a time.

There are other schools doing that work, as the call of God's mission has rung clearly through the ministry of many who teach, lighting a fire in most of the young people with Teach for America.

Others have lit fires in every single person who speaks hope and feeds and heals. Christians have grown mightily in their understanding that all we do, each interaction and every decision we make, can be part of healing and teaching and transforming the world into the kingdom of God.

That understanding is being nurtured in places like St. Hilda's House in New Haven, Connecticut—an intentional community seeking to serve God's mission. More and more young adults are listening well to Jesus's challenge to "just do it"—and leaving behind the trappings and baggage that so many others think are essential. Each one of us, as a Christian, is empowered and authorized to cast out demons—despair, ignorance, hate, poverty, fear, hunger—and heal a world filled with dis-ease. We have what we need, and Jesus walks with us.

The mission is simple: go out there and just do it.

Making Your Mark

What demons of injustice need to be cast out in your community? What demons of injustice threaten our larger communities—our nation and our world?

Traveling Light

What do you take with you when you travel? The last time I went overseas, I saw a family going to Brazil with two small children and about a dozen suitcases, boxes, and bags. They were trying to rearrange things so that nothing weighed more than fifty pounds.

I try to get what I need into a briefcase and a small carry-on suitcase, but when I have to take vestments and my pastoral staff, then I have to check a bag. The TSA folks think that stick is a weapon; they don't understand that it's intended to be a sign of peace and the end of division, not cause violence or hurt people. It's supposed to be a sign like the plowshares and pruning hooks Isaiah talks about (2:4). In any case, I don't get to travel as light as I would like to.

I've been reading about the Native Americans in what is now the southwestern United States and northern Mexico, in a book that tells what the annual migrations were like among the Comanches in the mid-1800s.[1] In warmer months, the hunters and warriors spent much of their time away from the villages, while the women, children, and elders did a lot of work processing buffalo and preserving food for winter. The great migrations to winter camps involved thousands of horses and long streams of people. Those great movements of people went on for centuries, until Spanish- and English-speaking settlers here and in Mexico arrived and began to farm and build houses, and until soldiers came to protect them and built forts. There weren't any fixed borders or fences until our immigrant ancestors built them.

The people who migrate across that border today carry little more than a small pack, with a bit of food, a few pieces of clothing, and a little water. They often run out of water in the deserts south of here. They come expecting to find hospitality among their friends and relatives who are already living in the United States. There are many tragedies along the way, yet those who come usually do find welcome among those who speak their language and share their heritage.

The difficulties for all travelers and migrants come from barriers, whether those are the great distance between here and Brazil, or the armed and fortified borders between Mexico and the countries south of it, or those borders between Mexico and the United States. Another kind of border exists in the divisions between cultures and nations and peoples—and that kind of border did exist between the Native American tribes. All those borders are what Paul is talking about in the letter to the Ephesians (2:13–22), when he says that Jesus has broken down the walls of hostility and division between people who have lived in different worlds.

Christians—as the Body of Christ—are a migrant company. We're on a journey toward a land where there will be no more war, on a mission to create a just world where there will be no more division or discrimination, where all kinds of walls will break down, where barriers no longer divide families, peoples, tribes, or nations. We're supposed to keep on traveling until we arrive there, and all God's people live together in peace.

Jesus sends his students out to search for that community, that promised land—but also to help build it (Luke 10:1–9). No one goes alone, and everyone travels light. It's not easy work, but it is simple and pretty straightforward—we're supposed to share food together and heal the sick. When we do that work of justice, we will indeed know that the kingdom of God has come near.

Why does Jesus tell his disciples, "Eat what they set before you, and don't move around from house to house"? Think about the last wedding feast you went to, or the last fiesta, or when a friend invited you to dinner. Did anybody leave because they didn't like the food? When we are rejoicing, and sharing the blessings that God has given, there usually isn't any place we'd rather be. Jesus reminds his friends that every meal, every encounter with friends or strangers, is supposed to be like God's great fiesta, the heavenly banquet.

Our job is to eat together, and to heal sickness and division. That justice work is why God sent Jesus among us. Illness or division of any kind keeps us from enjoying the great feast that God continues to set before us.

Traveling light is essential. If we're burdened with fifty-pound suitcases, our hands are already full and we won't be able to receive or enjoy whatever the next friend or stranger wants to share with us. It takes courage and faith to travel light, but it's also the most joyous way to go—and it removes the temptation to load ourselves with weapons or excess protection. It's radically countercultural in a consumerist society that thinks so highly of owning things, but it is the only real road to a community where the well-being of each person is the concern of all others. There's an African word for that understanding that individuals don't survive or thrive on their own—*ubuntu*. It is an understanding that our mutual welfare depends on how we care for every other person.

How can we help to heal the sickness and division right here in our own cities, states, and nations? The biggest barrier is fear—and some of it is well justified. It's very hard to think about sitting down to dinner with someone whose hands are filled with guns or whose mouth is full of violent words. That's why Jesus's words are so important: "Peace to this house." We have to begin in peace, not just putting down our sticks and insults, but setting aside the violence in our own hearts.

Traveling light has much to do with letting go of hate and the fear that usually accompanies it. We won't find the kingdom of God if our hearts or minds are filled with anything but the expectation of peace. It's not easy to let go of the anger, but it is possible. It helps to have a bigger view of what is possible, like this ancient dream of a world of peace. What kind of a world do we want for our children and grandchildren? We won't get there unless we can find the courage to go lightly, setting down the bitterness between us, and getting past the old divisions. It starts here, in our own hearts.

Will we set aside our anger? Will we let the swords be turned into tools for peace? Will we risk meeting a stranger, sitting down to eat together, and then work at building a bridge over that chasm between us? When we do, the kingdom of God has come near.

Making Your Mark

What baggage needs to be unloaded by our communities—and society at large—in order to break down the prejudice that underlies injustice? How can you personally travel more lightly to come closer to God and others?

Sharing the Wealth

—— ∽ ——

R emember the Kingston Trio singing "The Merry Minuet" in the
1960s? There was rioting, starvation, natural and human disaster
everywhere they looked—and everybody seemed to hate everybody
else. And the conclusion wasn't very promising, either:

> They're rioting in Africa. There's strife in Iran.
> What Nature doesn't do to us will be done by our
> Fellow Man.

It's abundantly obvious that almost all those realities are still with
us—even though lots of the players have changed and some of the
hated and hating nations no longer even exist.

Yet the hatred of one group toward another and the ongoing
reality of natural disasters both continue. Governments exist to
deal with those realities. Much of the appropriate work of governments is about defending the defenseless and limiting the ability of
the powerful to exploit the weak.

The biblical tradition is a long search for right and healed
relationships between human beings and God, for justice within
human communities. We don't ever hear of a completely right and
just community after Adam and Eve leave the garden, but we do
hear plenty of insistent reminders about repairing relationships
and correcting injustice.

In the book of Deuteronomy, there's a succinct summary of what
good government looks like: It "is not partial and takes no bribe,

who executes justice for the orphan and the widow, and who loves the strangers, providing them food and clothing" (10:17–21).

The repeated prophetic refrain from Israel, from Jesus, and from early Christian communities is about justice and caring for orphans, widows, and sojourners. When human communities are dealing justly with the needs of those who don't have social power, then strife, division, and war are usually far away. The divine dream of shalom, or the reign of God, is about people having enough to eat—and enough for a feast—and shelter, meaningful work, a place in community, access to healing, and the ability to live in peace. The story is told in many different ways: Isaiah's banquet on the hillside, with rich food and well-aged wines, where no one grieves anymore; images of the blind healed, the lame jumping for joy, and prisoners set free; Zechariah's vision of the old sitting in the streets of the city, while children play all around them, and all people live to a ripe and productive old age. War, hate, and the threat of violence make each version of that vision impossible. Most of the human evil of hatred and violence has its roots in self-centeredness. That's really the crux of human sin, whether it's the pettiness of *me first* in the food line, or the idolatry of insisting that I and the people in my in-group are lords of the universe. When God is at the center of our reality, and not we ourselves, we begin to see others in a more appropriate and deserving and loving light. Deciding to treat others as we want to be treated is love in action. Justice is simply love at work in the public square.

Jesus modeled that reality over and over again. His first public act was to read the prophet Isaiah's vision in the synagogue: "The spirit of the Lord is upon me, to bring good news to the poor, release to the captives, sight to the blind, to let the oppressed go free, and proclaim the year of the Lord's favor" (Luke 4:17–19, my summary). He spent his public ministry feeding, healing, and teaching people about the reality of God's dream. He did his own share of prophetic work, turning over the tables of moneychangers in the temple, challenging the injustices of both religious and political governments, and seeking to protect and build up the weak. He proclaimed the kingdom of God as those who care for the least of these: the hungry, thirsty, naked, homeless, sick, and imprisoned—and strangers (Matthew 25:37–40).

Where are we most grievously distant from the divine vision of a healed community? The most basic issue of food and hunger is a sign and symbol of the ways in which we are collectively failing to care for the least of these. A billion people are hungry across the globe, and the number has grown 10 percent in the last couple of years due to steeply rising food prices and global recession. Hunger differentially affects the most vulnerable—children, the poor, single and mostly female parents, minimum wage workers, Native Americans on reservations. Across the globe, 70 percent of the hungry are women and girls, usually in societies where they have little or no access to political power.[1]

Over fifty million people are hungry in the United States—one person in six, one child in four.[2] Children who suffer from hunger do much more poorly in school, and indeed, longitudinal studies (like the ones which followed the Dutch famine in the Second World War) show multigenerational effects of inadequate nutrition. Basic human dignity, and basic justice, should insist that everyone be afforded an adequate diet. We will not all live in peace until everyone has enough to eat.

Our own citizens are hungry, and even though some try to respond, there is active resistance even to the simple act of feeding people. There was a powerful article in the New York Times not long ago about attempts to feed people in a park in Florida being foiled by the arrest of volunteers who were handing out food.[3] They didn't have a city permit, and groups can only get two permits per year to feed people—that's for a total of two meals per year. Hackers were responding, shutting down the websites of the city, the mayor's re-election campaign, the Fraternal Order of Police, and a city redevelopment organization.

We see only slightly more subtle resistance to feeding people in Congress, where farm subsidies are routinely privileged over food subsidies. Recent action by the House cut food assistance to Women, Infants, and Children (WIC) by 13 percent, and international food aid by a third, while declining to limit the subsidies provided to farmers. It also cut out funding for local food initiatives—the kind that encourage people to learn where their food comes from, and to meet the farmers in their area.

We spend far more on military operations than on feeding the hungry, perhaps not recognizing that in the long term war only produces more people who are hungry, ill, displaced, widowed, or orphaned. A quarter of the 2012 federal budget was designated for defense. Food aid for the hungry within the United States constituted about 3 percent of that budget, and a paltry 0.04 of 1 percent was proposed for international food assistance.[4] Even so, over the last several decades, real progress has been made in reducing hunger both in the United States and overseas. We were moving in the right direction before the recession began in 2008.

There have been proposals in the Senate to cap discretionary spending—among other things, to limit the amount that can be spent on programs that feed people, and to require that all such programs be cut by a fixed percentage. That would decimate foreign food aid and require major cuts in domestic food assistance.

There are many interrelated reasons for our current economic woes. They cannot be remedied by starving the hungry. We have more than enough wealth in the United States to feed those who are hungry here, and a small portion of that spending would go a very long way toward relieving starvation across the globe. When the MDGs were first proposed, the developed nations of the world agreed to dedicate a small fraction of 1 percent of their gross national incomes to relieving the worst of global poverty. The

Scandinavian nations and a couple of others in Europe have met or exceeded their promises. The United States has provided less than half of what was promised.

We live in a nation that has the highest income disparity in the world. Argentina is our only close peer. From 1940 until the early 1980s, the wealthiest 10 percent of Americans received about a third of the nation's income. Since then, that share has grown to nearly half the income. The top 1 percent now receive 21 percent of the nation's income, a figure that's doubled in the last thirty years. The top 0.1 percent take in nearly 8 percent of the nation's income, and that has quadrupled in the last thirty years.[5]

We have one biblical image after the garden of Eden in which nobody's hungry—it might be called the garden of Even. The story comes from Jerusalem, that city of dreams, in the first years of the post-Easter Christian community:

> Now the whole group of those who believed were of one heart and soul, and no one claimed private owner-ship of any possessions, but everything they owned was held in common. With great power the apostles gave their testimony to the resurrection of the Lord Jesus, and great grace was upon them all. *There was not a needy person among them,* for as many as owned lands or houses sold them and brought the proceeds of what was sold. They laid it at the apostles' feet, and it was distributed to each as any had need.
>
> (ACTS 4:32–35, EMPHASIS ADDED)

That kind of community, rooted in justice, has rarely existed since, and none has lasted very long. Yet we are unlikely to find peace or stability as long as the haves keep increasing their share, and others live in want. We have a dream for the kind of government that might permit a reduction in the number of needy and hungry: "who is not partial and takes no bribe, who executes justice for the orphan and the widow, and who loves the strangers, providing them food and clothing" (Deuteronomy 10:17–18).

That is what it looks like to live as good and godly people. Government is meant to be a servant of the governed. What will the governed—all of us—do about widows, and orphans, and strangers? Our part in God's mission is to work toward a world that looks more like that early Christian "garden of Even."

Making Your Mark

What are you doing at the very local level to feed the hungry? What can you do at larger scales, through your work as a citizen—in advocacy with legislators, organizing with others, and with your vote?

Living in Joyful Hope

What do you hope for? What holy dream keeps you searching in the midst of darkness? I don't mean a list for Santa Claus, but we could all learn something from the earnestness and energy of childlike anticipation. Most of us adults are too shy or fearful or even ashamed to name our big and lasting hopes. We make do with lesser pursuits, like shopping for things that won't answer our hopes for more than an instant.

Christian communities are places of hope. We're all in the same boat—we're looking for home, we want to belong, we want to be valued, we want to be welcomed in a place of safety and warmth by people who love us. Once we get a little experience of that, we just might have enough courage to go on back out there and get to work on our deepest, most fervent hopes. We gather as a community to catch a glimpse of a dream that's big enough and encouraging enough to begin to drive out fear and where we can begin to experience a deep and abiding and transforming hope.

The prophet Isaiah broadcasts hope to a people who are lost, depressed, and feeling abandoned. He wrote three thousand years ago to Israelites who were far from home, but those exiles in Babylon are a lot like us, for we all live as strangers in a land we didn't choose—economic downturn, government that doesn't work as it should for the good of all, people afraid of unemployment or not having access to medical care, never being quite sure that we're good enough or loved enough. Isaiah tells his fellow Israelites to dream big, because

God is eventually going to heal all of that, and he's going to send them a good king faithful to their relationship with God, God's going to install a government that will bring peace to the people and justice to the nation (Isaiah 11:1–10).

Many people are quite surprised by how much the biblical prophets talk about good government—and it's related to why Jesus is called Wisdom's prophet. The language in the gospels about Jesus as Lord is a direct contrast and challenge to Caesar as Lord, and it's a commentary on the unjust government that Jesus and his neighbors are experiencing. When you think about government in Chicago, or in your city, or nation, what do you hope for?

When we gather together in worship, especially during the season of Advent, the scripture readings we listen to are dripping with hope—consider the psalmist's hope for a good and just king (Psalm 72), and Paul's insistence in his letter to the Romans that all of the scriptures are written to give hope. He reminds his community in Rome that a new shoot from the root of Jesse will bring hope for all the nations, and not just Israel (Romans 15:4–13). And in the gospel, John the Baptist, challenging his neighbors to "Repent, the kingdom of heaven has come near," is really saying something like, "Turn around and start down a new road, because a better government is coming, a divine one, rooted in justice, not corruption" (Matthew 3:1–12). His language gets pretty confrontational—prophets aren't always filled with sweetness and light—and he takes on the religious leaders by demanding to know why they're running away. They can't just keep on going through the same religious motions and expect to be part of the hope that is coming: "Who warned you to flee?" Why are you running away, when what the world has hoped for is coming?

Those Pharisees and Sadducees who were running away may not have wanted to think about better government—it was easier to focus on the details of religious forms in their own lives. Transformation that leads to new relationships and just government is challenging. Maybe we're afraid of transformation, too.

If we can't touch our own deep fears, then maybe we can listen to all the public communication around us that's filled with doom and gloom. The great majority of Americans are afraid of not being able to make it. Unemployment in the United States is hovering around 9 percent, but there are at least another 15 to 20 percent who are underemployed or still not making enough to support themselves, particularly if they are male, minority, younger, or less educated. Foreclosure rates are distressingly high, bankruptcy filings have increased. The United States and many other nations are in the midst of unprecedented budget cuts, which will hurt most those least able to survive them.

Where is hope in the face of statistics like that? What keeps us from running away like the leaders John the Baptist took on, or burying our heads in the sand? The answer lies in why we gather in faith communities—our yearning to be part of that ridiculous, absurd expectation that a better rule is possible. We have lots of companions in our irrational hope that sweeping changes are coming.

Everywhere I've looked recently, I've seen hope. The hospice patient I saw knows that the waning days of his life have meaning, he's grateful for his wife of fifty years, he's giving thanks for the blessing of the sun's warmth, and he's hopeful for what is coming. The healing ministries of the hospitals I've visited, and the passion of those who work there to find new partnerships to serve the sick and injured bring hope to everyone they touch. Community organizations are bringing hope to children and adults through decent and dignified housing at affordable rents, and growing ministries around the country are building bridges between English speakers and Spanish speakers, recent immigrants and the great-great-great-grandchildren of immigrants, speaking hope to strangers in a strange land.

And I've also met a remarkable group of eight young adults who exude hope—the Julians, who live together in community, offering their gifts in service in several ministries, exploring their faith and their vocation.[1] The saint for whom this group is named, Julian of Norwich, lived in a small stone room set between the world and a parish church, with windows into each. Her counsel offered hope and strength to many visitors, and she is probably best remembered for reminding us that "all will be well, and all will be well, and all manner of thing shall be well." Hope makes all things possible. That hope can transform the structures of this world into the "good government" that Isaiah expected and Jesus taught us to pray for. Hope is what it means to say that Jesus is Lord and not Caesar. Hope means that we really do expect the reign of God, on earth as it is in heaven.

Yet that kind of hope requires enough vulnerability to own our fears. We can't really hope unless we know what's wrong. When we can begin to name and acknowledge those fears, we'll find that hope is the cure. Hope—holy hope, even holy hope-filled boldness—is the only known antidote for fear, depression, boredom, abandonment, lostness, exile, grief. Hope is what our faith demands, and offers. We wait and work and yearn for light in the darkness and for the prince of peace. If we can name the fear, hope will blow in like the wind under the door, transforming everything in its path.

Making Your Mark

What signs of hope for a transformed world—both large and small—have you encountered?

PART V

The Fifth Mark of Mission

To Strive to Safeguard the Integrity of Creation, and Sustain and Renew the Life of the Earth

One Body

As Christians, we gather as many sorts and kinds and conditions of people, with varying languages and positions and opinions. Yet all of us know one Lord, one faith, one baptism, and we claim one God and father of us all. It is a blessing, and a miracle, that we can claim our unity as often and deeply as we do.

Think about the bodies each one of us inhabits. Those bodies are made up of trillions of cells, working together most of the time to keep the whole thing reasonably intact and healthy. If your body suffers an affront, like falling down and skinning your knee, many parts go to work immediately to stop the bleeding, mobilize to defend you from germs that might infect that knee, and start cleaning up the damage. The muscles and nerves around the scrape get sore, which serves in part to keep you from overusing your knee until it's well on the road to healing.

Yet that system we call a body is a whole lot more complex and interconnected than we usually recognize. It's made up of many different kinds of cells, not all of which have our unique DNA. We have lots of other kinds of life in and on us—like mites, that are usually too small to see; bacteria, viruses, fungi, and maybe even some other things that we might call parasites. But most of those other forms of life are essential to our well-being. The bacteria in our guts help us digest food and absorb nutrients. The little energy machines in our cells called mitochondria were probably originally a different form of life. We know that because all the ones we have are descended from the ones in our mother's egg. The great miracle is that most of the time this immensely complex system of members works together for our health and healing. Most of that system works unconsciously, far from being controlled by conscious thought, although we *can* cooperate with it in seeking a healthier state. Or we can choose not to cooperate, by overeating, under-exercising, or using excessive stuff (like antibiotics) that kills the good bacteria and fungi in our guts or on our skin.

The same principles apply to the larger body of God's creation, whether we talk about just the human part of creation or the whole planet. Human history is filled with episodes of one group trying to sanitize its environment by eliminating another part of the body. National Socialism—Nazism—is a demonic icon of that, but there's no shortage of examples in recent years: the internecine slaughter in Rwanda; the struggles in Abyei, on the border between northern and southern Sudan; the struggle between Israelis and Palestinians, or North and South Korea; or the repeated spasms of violence in the United States between people of different ethnic origins. One part of the body seeks to eliminate another, and the health—and holiness—of humanity in that part of the world is diminished. The sickness can be fatal—for individuals, communities, and even nations.

Yet we do see counter-examples, where the immune system is strong enough to permit health in two parts of the body that don't readily recognize each other. It's a very short time frame, but the referendum in Sudan forming the new entity of South Sudan gives beginning evidence of a healthy self-differentiation, rather than descending into full-scale war. When communities begin to find a common identity and purpose, the whole body enjoys much greater health.

The sickness or dis-ease that results from attempts to expunge the *other* can last for generations, as well as decrease the viability of the whole system. *Empire of the Summer Moon* tells about the struggle over the Texas frontier between the Comanche bands and both English- and Spanish-speaking settlers. It's a microcosm of the struggle between native peoples and European settlers seeking their "manifest destiny." The whole body is still suffering—native peoples from poverty, suicide, cultural extinction, and hopelessness; the heirs of the settlers from blindness about relationship to a larger body; and the non-human creation from the destruction of the buffalo, the native prairie, and the assumption that other crops could easily and appropriately displace native ones. The poverty in many rural areas has some connection to the same processes.

We're all sick in some degree because of our disconnection from the larger body of God's whole creation. Almost everyone forgot, ignored, or never learned what it means to be part of one body, intended to live in peace and harmony with all the other parts of the body. We're still paying the price, especially in our lack of awareness of our impact on the rest of creation. What we dig and pipe out of the earth is changing our long-term expectations for flourishing or even surviving on this planet.

Yet God continues to remind us that we are all members of one body, and that that body is supposed to be a bringer of good news to the oppressed, a comfort to those in mourning, and a deliverer of captives. We're supposed to bring praise, rather than crush spirits. We're reminded over and over again that we will be given what we need, and that together we can do what no one part can accomplish. This Body of Christ is meant to be the healer of nations, whether Haiti or Navajo or Sudan or the United States.

What gets in the way? Our tendency to act like killer T cells, those important white blood cells that run around our bodies looking for invaders, those awful buggers that aren't us! Sometimes the better response is the slower one—lest we mistake an unfamiliar life form for an enemy. What's causing this fever—is it a cholera bacterium, or is it a stray Pentecostal? I'm not suggesting that we cozy up to cholera, but test and moderate our response until we're certain—because the response is often more destructive than the unexpected visitor. That's what allergies are, and most of the autoimmune diseases—overreactions to other parts of the body of God's creation.

Spiritual discipline is designed to moderate our allergic response to foreigners. Jesus's words in that gospel are about discerning the difference between fish and eggs and scorpions and snakes. Knocking, asking, and seeking are all ways of slowing down the overreaction (Luke 11:9–13).

We are all members of one body, that of God's creation. The important truth is that we need all these parts, even if we do have allergic reactions to some of them, because God's vision of a healed world isn't possible without all the members working together as a whole. Haiti right now is a good example, as is Japan, and Christchurch, New Zealand. In each place where the fabric of the earth has been torn apart, the fabric of relationships has been damaged as well. The larger body of God's creation will be healed as we work together to serve the healing of each nation. In truth, God's creation will only be healed when each member of the body knows good news, healing, and deliverance.

Making Your Mark

What bodies are you a member of? Which ones need healing? Where do you see allergic reactions to other members of those bodies?

In the Garden

———— ∽∽∽∽ ————

I travel a lot, and it seems that everywhere I go, there's a glimpse of the glory of God.

Climbing mountains is a pretty significant way to encounter the glory of God. Have you ever been up on the mountain, like Moses, awestruck at the wonder of what God is up to?

Not long ago, leaving a meeting in Ecuador, I could see a small circular rainbow below us, tracking the plane's progress across the desert of South America. I've only seen one other rainbow like that, as I was flying a small plane directly toward a dark and foreboding storm cloud. It brought me both comfort and promise. This planet is filled with the glory of God, if we're ready to look for the creator's creativity.

That meeting was in the capital city of Quito. More than two million people live there—almost a seventh of Ecuador's wonderfully diverse population. The city itself is set in a mountain valley three kilometers high, with snow-covered volcanoes in the distance. God's creativity was very much in evidence.

Yet the glory of God's creativity was also evident in the work we did together there—learning about the realities of migration, climate change, poverty, and the burden of debt in the Latin American context. We reflected on the ways in which God's creative word is emerging to address those realities in different liberation theologies. I know the same is happening around the world—and theologies of liberation have been a significant part of the church's role in the struggle against apartheid in South Africa and the struggle over relationships between descendants of European colonizers and indigenous populations, conflict over land use and resource extraction, and migration from neighboring countries driven by poverty and violence in Latin America. God's creativity is abundantly evident in human responses to massive human challenges.

In South Africa, I went on pilgrimage to Robben Island, where anti-apartheid activists were imprisoned near Cape Town. The glory of God was much in evidence there, both in the beauty of that environment on a brisk spring day and in the stories about the inmates' persistent hope over the centuries. Robben Island is now a World Heritage Site, a kind of living museum, and we saw evidence of that hope in the joy-filled letters Robert Subukwe, a South African political dissident, wrote to his wife, in the paper and books made from cement bags that prisoners used to teach and equip others for the work of transformation, and in the gardens emerging from former prison yards. Many of South Africa's leaders were formed in that creative crucible, and many more around the world have been inspired by it.

Earlier I mentioned a Christian named Irenaeus who famously said that the glory of God is a human being fully alive. When God's creatures are filled with creative energy, God's glory does indeed become most alive and evident. When we are passionately invested as partners in that creativity, we are becoming more of who and what God created us to be. Jesus speaks of that same kind of passion when he tells of the sons asked to work in the vineyard (Matthew 21:28–32). Both were sent, but only one answered the call by actually going to work. Which one of us will answer that passionate call to creative labor in God's vineyard?

The vineyard is all around us—it's an ancient image of creation, ready to become fruitful and life-giving. Israel is often called God's vineyard or God's planting. The only question is whether we're willing to cooperate, to co-create. Who will go and work in the vineyard? We may say yes, like the first brother in that parable, and not ever start. Or we may decline the invitation at first, like the second brother did, yet eventually get moving in spite of ourselves. But for most of us, the challenge has more to do with figuring out just what working in the vineyard means.

The answer has to do with the glory of being fully alive. Another word for that aliveness is passion. What really gets us moving? What gets our blood racing and our spirit soaring and heart singing? It's not the same thing for everyone, and doing it usually has a significant element of sacrifice as well as joy. We become holy (which is what sacrifice means) in doing what makes us most fully alive.

Awe at the natural environment stirs most people who live close to the land or who learn to appreciate the unconstructed world. That sense of the holiness of creation is part of the spirituality of most indigenous peoples, and it is leading more and more people of faith to challenge the abuse of creation, our waste of its gifts, and our wanton destruction of its blessing. It was shocking to see how much garbage there was in the water on the way over to Robben Island. It's also clear that fresh water is a precious resource on that island. The prisoners' gardens on that sandy bit of land often dried up for lack of summer water, and so do the township vegetable gardens in the nearby Cape Flats. Our changing planet will make it harder and harder for the poorest among us to survive those summer droughts—as well as expanding the range of malarial mosquitoes and diminishing the quantity of arable land. Who will go work in that garden? Who will challenge those who misuse or waste the vineyard?

Once we start to get our hands dirty, we begin to see that the state of the vineyard or the garden affects all of God's creation, and that the same vulnerable populations are still suffering just as much as they did in Moses's day—the widows, orphans, immigrants, the landless. The rich can move, the wealthy can pay higher prices for shrinking amounts of water and food, the powerful can build stronger houses to avoid the cruelest of changing weather patterns.

When I was in South Africa I went out with others to Khayelit-sha, an impoverished township near Cape Town, for a celebration of the work of HOPE Africa in tending to the forgotten and the vulnerable—those who are infected with AIDS, the orphans, and the elders who care for them. Hope comes from labor in the vine-yard—tending the vine, fertilizing it, pruning it. One of the young girls who danced at the celebration said to me, "We're poor. That's why we're dancing—so people will help us." God's ability to lure new life into being happens in the midst of human beings, both as individuals and in community. It may begin without our conscious awareness, but at some point our participation is necessary. That girl is learning to voice a cry for justice, even as she brings hope to her neighbors.

What's our part of the vineyard? Is it tending the soil, ensuring adequate water, digging out the weeds? Or have we been invited to prune the wild growth out of the vineyard? Fertile soil always invites weeds, and if they're left alone, they eventually steal all the nutrients from the soil. Human communities without caretakers experience the same thing—the weedy behavior we call exploitation or greed or corruption. The human vineyard needs gardeners of justice, so that tender growth is protected, so that fruit is shared and no one outside the gate goes hungry.

The glory of God is all around us, but we're usually only able to see glimpses of it. We wait for the coming of God's reign, and that ancient dream of shalom, to see it in its fullness. Yet each time we answer "yes" and go work in the garden, we begin to see that glory in the fertility of the soil, in the hope for bountiful harvests to feed the whole community, in the partnership of other gardeners, and in the discipline we call justice, ensuring that no one gets fat while some go hungry. Each part of that work begins to transform the earth into the vineyard, and pasture, and garden that yields Isaiah's mountain picnic: a feast of rich food and well-aged wines, strained clear (Isaiah 25:6–10). And God will pull away the pall of death that is cast over all peoples, like the "tablecloth" (which is what residents of Cape Town call the cloud that rests on their local mountain) rising from Table Mountain. The Lord will wipe away tears and grief, and God's people will live together in peace.

Who will go and work in the vineyard? When we do, we are certain to find the glory of God, and to experience it in willing and passionate and courageous people, fully alive.

Making Your Mark

Where have you seen the glory of God passing by? What garden are you being called to work in?

Healing the Body
of God

———⟋⟋⟋⟋⟍———

We are far more interconnected than we have ever been—and we are more deeply aware of our connections. The image born of chaos science, that a butterfly's wingbeats in China may affect the course of a storm in the Gulf of Mexico, is daily reality if we will only notice. For those who gather as interconnected parts of the Body of Christ, that understanding is foundational to our faith. There is an even deeper and more pervasive understanding of our interconnectedness—the whole of God's creation, which Sallie McFague has written about in *The Body of God: An Ecological Theology*. A careful examination of our shared theology within the Christian family invites us to remember that the saving work of Jesus of Nazareth has implications for all that God has made. Our common work must be concerned with all of creation, all of humanity, and all people of faith.

Our interconnectedness is becoming evident not just in instantaneous communications or the rapid spread of pandemics around the globe, but in the very real consequences of oil spills off the shores of the United States on those who live hundreds or thousands of miles away. We are beginning to understand that pumping carbon into the earth's atmosphere is increasing the melting of glaciers in Greenland and the Antarctic, and the rising level of the oceans that results is beginning to submerge the homelands of Kiribati in the Pacific and Bangladesh in southern Asia. Our use of additives in food, antibiotics in commercial dairy and meat production, and the panoply of synthetic compounds in our daily lives are beginning to impact the reproductive biology of human beings around the globe—as well as the fish in our backyard streams. Violence in one part of the globe is easily exported to surrounding nations as well as to those at a distance. The economic storm of the past few years has had repercussions on human society far beyond its origins on the exchanges of Wall Street, London, or Hong Kong—and beyond the capacity of individual governments expected to regulate the commerce of their own nations.

We are all interconnected in ways that we are only beginning to understand incarnationally. This body of God has many, many parts, and the ancient prophetic dream of a healed world expects those parts to work together for the glory of God and the benefit of the whole.

Our task as Christians in the coming decades will be more challenging than ever, and the task will need all our varied and unique gifts. The voices of people of faith must be a prophetic source for lasting change that moves toward healing the body of God. If we can begin to affirm our place in that body of God, in concert with other people of faith, both Christian and not, we will discover that the Holy One has been here before us.

The God we worship, whose son we follow, is luring us into an unexpected and radically open future. The question is whether we have courage to try new ways, to build a world where economies are understood as servants of all human beings rather than a few, where economic systems contribute to the health and prosperity of a far wider swath of humanity. The challenges of greed, and the idolatry of power and wealth, are not new, but the contexts in which we live will require new methods to address them. Local solutions are no longer enough; we must think globally, we must consider the whole body of God, not simply our local congregations or single denominations, nations, or faith traditions.

There is an immensely urgent example in the current anxiety in Sudan. The Comprehensive Peace Agreement, negotiated in 2005 with the assistance of other nations, including the United States, brought about a referendum in January of 2011, permitting the southern Sudanese to decide their future—whether to remain connected to the Khartoum government and northern Sudan, or to gain their independence as a separate nation. The added complexities include the fact that most of the Khartoum government's financial resources come from the sale of oil, two-thirds of which is in southern Sudan. At least two million southern Sudanese live as IDPs (internally displaced persons) in northern Sudan. There are religious and tribal differences compounding the divisions, for most of the north is Muslim and the south is primarily Christian or practices native African religion. The environmental destruction and human displacement over the last two decades of war have caused untold misery. Violence continues, though at lower levels than before the Comprehensive Peace Agreement (CPA). Now, after the referendum to form the new nation of South Sudan, churches and NGOs are working together to ease the transition and to avoid the possibility of another bloodbath like the one that occurred in similar circumstances in Rwanda in the 1990s.

The role of churches is to be a witness to Jesus's saving work on behalf of all creation. It is only as God's body, reaching across not only Christian difference, but into the hearts and hands of our interfaith partners, that we have any possibility of joining Jesus's witness on behalf of the least of these. The situation on the US Gulf Coast following Katrina required a similar urgent clamor by people of faith, as has the aftermath of Haiti's earthquake. Moving toward God's shalom requires our active and urgent response.

Will we be witnesses of these things? Will we become witnesses who join the lament of wanderers in the desert and the widow seeking justice? We can look and not see, listen and not hear, or we can witness and act in solidarity with our sisters and brothers as part of the body of God.

Making Your Mark

Where do you see the body of God in need of healing? Where might you look for partners in that work?

Transforming
the Planet

J esus may have said that we will always have the poor with us,
but he himself made the poor a central part of his own work. He
spent much of his public ministry feeding, healing, and teaching
the crowds who followed him. Those crowds were almost certainly
the homeless or landless, who had little opportunity for economic
stability or what today we would call food security. He challenged
both political and religious governments about the injustices of
taxation policy and realities that made the rich richer and the poor
poorer. The 2008 presidential election in the United States was
not the first time somebody figured out that Jesus was a community organizer.

At their best, communities of Christians have served the poor by
focusing on the same basic issues of food, healing, housing, education, employment, and the structural injustices that keep people in
poverty. Those basic human needs and rights are no different today
than they were in first-century Palestine, and the lack of a productive connection to land is still a central issue in poverty.

That work grows out of the cosmic dream of a healed world—
shalom or the reign of God—a society in which no one goes hungry, and everyone has enough for a feast, where premature death is
largely unknown and illness is answered with healing, in which the
structural injustices have been remedied so there are no impulses to
war, and all are free to live in peace. That dream includes a healed
planet as well, where the gifts of creation are honored and people

work together to safeguard the integrity of the earth. We live in hope for a world redeemed into that reality, and we work at transformation because we are a very long way indeed from seeing it come to fruition.

Transformation of communities—and indeed the entire planet—begins with what you might remember theologian Nelle Morton calling "hearing people into speech."[1] Speech is creative, beginning with the divine version in Genesis' first creation story, in which God speaks each part of the cosmos into existence: "God said, 'let there be light'… and God said, 'let the waters be gathered together, and let the dry land appear,' and God said, 'let the earth put forth vegetation,'—and speech becomes reality (Genesis 1). To Morton, the act of hearing is like the story of creation—beginning with a space, and a receptive environment in which speech can emerge. The act of voicing one's lament or joy is creative, and the art of hearing others into speech underlies community organizing. When the difference between current reality and that cosmic dream can be named, and heard, transformation has begun.

Some remarkable work of transformation is ongoing in cities and communities around the world. When I served in Nevada, I had the opportunity to visit Kenya as we sought to build mission partnerships with three dioceses there. It was my first real taste of significant city organizing. A number of church-related groups were working in Nairobi's biggest slum, Kibera. Kibera began as returning soldiers were given plots after the First World War. The settlement was later deemed illegal by the post-independence Kenyan government. Much of the systemic injustice in places like Kibera has to do with lack of access to the earth and its resources: clean water, fertile soil, enough healthy environmental resources to cope with human waste and garbage.

Part of the mission toward a healed world calls Christians to take seriously the care and nurture of entire communities, and, indeed, the entire planet. How often do we listen to the groaning of the earth, and the communicable diseases that we human beings are spreading across the globe? I don't mean AIDS or SARS, but the diseases of blind consumption and thoughtless waste. Creation is groaning in travail, waiting for the children of God to grow up into the full stature of Christ (Ephesians 4:13–16) and to start loving their neighbors as themselves. As the population of this planet continues to grow almost exponentially, and an increasing proportion removes to urban environments, the challenges of city living will only continue to increase. Today's major slums will soon seem an easy redevelopment project compared to the inadequately fed and housed millions who congregate in cities hoping for employment, education, and some possibility of living—hoping for hope.

Cities will be massively affected by climate change. We are seeing those realities already in the aftermath of Katrina, in the flooding along the Mississippi, and in the tornadoes that have afflicted not only Tornado Alley but even cities in the Northeast. Densely populated areas are more vulnerable to natural disasters, not only earthquakes but those disasters that grow in severity with increasing climatic change. The poorest are the most affected. Just as the lower Ninth Ward was more vulnerable to flooding in New Orleans, residents of mobile homes have died at far higher rates in recent tornadoes than residents in more substantial and expensive housing.

Increasing population densities will differentially disadvantage the poorest. That is a structural injustice that must be addressed through advocacy and societal change as well as direct, hands-on ministries of care and healing. The other pressing structural challenge concerns the widening economic gap, in the United States and across the globe. Climate change, coupled with present economic realities, is sending burgeoning economic powers like China far abroad, looking for farmland. The appetite for fuel continues to grow, adding to the social inequity and instability in almost all cities.

As the rates of consumption in the developed world show little sign of abating, who will go and speak for us? The resistance to change is legion. The biggest obstacle seems to be the lack of hope for prompting effective change. If new possibilities are coming to the authoritarian states of Africa and the Middle East, beginning in the Arab Spring of 2011, then change is certainly possible in the developed West and North. We need bold and prophetic voices, we need networks of inspired and organized people, and we need that vision of a healed world of peace and justice for all. There is abundant work to be done, yet it must always be inspired by that vision of shalom and salaam—food and drink for feasting, dignified work and Sabbath leisure, none lording it over another, all God's children living in peace. God sends us as Christians to pray that it may be so—and to work like hell to make it so.

Making Your Mark

What sorts of organizing are needed to address the differential vulnerabilities in our cities? What can you be doing in your own city?

Networks for
the Future

Perhaps the largest and most significant issue of justice facing us as people of faith has to do with our care of the garden in which God has planted us. The ways we use or abuse the gifts of creation are potential occasions either of sin or co-creative redemption. They also have cosmic consequence, for the lives of all human beings and all other creatures on the planet are affected by the decisions we make. Those decisions also have implications for the lives of the human beings and other creatures who will follow us. Our Christian tradition has not given us great resources or encouragement for considering the lives of those who follow us, yet they too must be considered as fellow or potential members of the communion of saints. We are connected to those who will follow us, just as we are connected to those who have come before. Our Native American brothers and sisters have something to teach us: The ethical calculus of many tribal traditions considers the seven generations before and the seven generations yet to come. We are all connected in a vast network.

We are beginning to understand, for example, that our use of fossil fuels, and our consumption-based economies are rapidly depriving the peoples of the South Pacific of their homelands, and rapidly defrosting the homelands of the peoples of the Arctic. The broad ecosystems in both regions are being changed in ways beyond the members' ability to adapt. The people of the Pacific islands of Kiribati and Tuvalu will likely have to move to higher ground within a few short years, and they've begun to negotiate for land in higher countries. The Gwich'in peoples of the Alaskan and Canadian Arctic will lose their food source, culture, and communities as the caribou find it harder to migrate through thawed tundra. Other Arctic peoples are losing their ability to hunt and fish as sea ice recedes. The Alaskan community of Kivalina is rapidly being eroded by storms, for sea ice no longer protects its shoreline. Recent reports of large methane plumes in the Arctic, from melting deposits of methane hydrides, are likely to vastly complicate and exacerbate atmospheric warming, for methane is a much more destructive greenhouse gas than carbon dioxide.

Our connections are apparent in the United States as well. We are seeing the pressures of water scarcity, long known in the West, exacerbated as more and more water is withdrawn by thirsty populations and inappropriate farming techniques upstream. No single religious community is large enough, gifted enough, or extensive enough to respond to these challenges. We can only begin to do so in communion with a larger network of God's human family, with people of faith of all sorts, who seek a healed and more just world. We will be faithless if we fail to share the good news of God's reign by working with all possible partners in seeking a truly universal response to God's mission to heal this world, to restore all that is to right relationship with God, and each other.

As Christians, our mission is to be instruments of God's salvation—or healing—of the world. It's easy for us to spiritualize what that means. One of the great heretical tendencies of the West has been just that—insisting that salvation is only about the individual, rather than her and his place in the larger society. The baptized are gathered into a body, and even though each is healed in his or her own person, that healing is only possible in the larger body, and it is meant for the healing and the greater life of all creation.

We must insist that Jesus's life, ministry, death, and resurrection had—and have—consequences for the entirety of what is, that his work set the created order forward on the journey homeward into God. The constant peril is thinking too small.

But God's mission challenges us to think big, as we seek to partner with faith communities around the globe on issues of climate change and environmental justice. The nerve cells in these interfaith networks are growing faster than in other places, perhaps because we share a sense of urgency about the mission to heal creation.

Networks are a powerful counterforce to the charity or colonial models that have too often characterized Christian mission. We are beginning to heal from some of that unidirectional kind of mission work as we discover that the dependencies it fosters are in the long term only destructive. Those colonial models grew out of an arrogance about supposedly superior gifts, and they are healed or corrected through discovering the gifts of the poor and of the other. Perhaps first among those gifts is the radical understanding of dependence on God for all of life—an awareness easy to miss in the midst of wealth, control, and competence in outward things. The end of Christendom in the West is bringing us back to a much earlier, radical (from the roots of our faith) understanding of our utter dependence on God, and our interdependence as fellow human beings for the health of all creation.

Our own health equally depends on the health of this planet. There is likely no other mission field so globally important, and so influential on the other spheres of mission. Climate change is already making the lives of the poorest harder. Crop yields of wheat, corn, and soybeans are already showing small decreases related to changed weather patterns. In the last couple of years, we've seen increased hunger in Africa because of the shift toward growing grain and corn for biofuels rather than for food. Water is fast becoming the new critical resource, and it is most difficult to obtain in the poorest parts of the world. We have made some progress toward achieving the Millenium Development Goals, but some of that progress is already being eroded by these worsening climatic realities. When there is little water, who must walk hours to fetch it? Most often, it's the girls who should be in school, and their mothers who have few other options. We will not achieve the Millennium Goal of full education for girls as well as boys, nor the goal of empowering women, nor the goal of ending hunger, without adequate water.

The consumerist economies of the West are based on the false gods of greed and ever-increasing growth. We are being consumed by those realities, and the resulting and growing chasm between rich and poor has biblical echoes of the cows of Bashan lolling on ivory couches (Amos 4:1). These are profoundly spiritual challenges, and the leadership of Christian communities, as well as all the partners we can discover and nurture, is needed in order to transform the future.

We must build networks for that transformed future, toward that image of the reign of God where no one is hungry, and all live at peace in abundantly fruitful orchards. That future is only possible with a network of interdependent relationships beyond our current understanding. We must reach beyond the bounds that divide us, for the love of God and our neighbors. We can do no less. We can do nothing more important.

Making Your Mark

Where are you discovering connections you were unaware of last year, or five years ago? How is that growing interdependence a gift for the transformation of God's world toward shalom? Who needs to be part of your ongoing discovery?

Notes

Introduction

1. See the Anglican Communion website, www.anglicancommunion.org/ministry/mission/fivemarks.cfm.
2. See "Doctrine of Discovery Resources" on The Episcopal Church website, www.episcopalchurch.org/page/doctrine-discovery-resources.
3. See www.indianetzone.com/35/first_phase_missionary_activities_british_india.htm.

Seeing the Face of Jesus

1. Baptismal Covenant, *The Book of Common Prayer* (New York: Church Hymnal Corporation, 1979), 305.

From the Upper Room to the Ends of the Earth

1. Called "apostle to the apostles" by the Orthodox, for she was first to announce the resurrection.

Archaeology of Hope

1. Randy Kennedy, "China Asks Penn to Remove All Artifacts From 'Silk Road' Exhibition," *New York Times*, 22 Feb 2011, Arts Beat.
2. Shannon Dihinny, "Oregon Tribes Pursue First Bison Hunt in Century" (New York: Associated Press, 2011).
3. Learn more about this story in the film *Pray the Devil Back to Hell.* (See www.praythedevilbacktohell.com/index.php).
4. Nelle Morton, *The Journey Is Home* (Boston: Beacon, 1985).

Blessing and Hope

1. *The Book of Common Prayer* (New York: Church Hymnal Corporation, 1979), 212.

Tweeting the Gospel

1. Article XXIV: It is a thing plainly repugnant to the Word of God, and the custom of the Primitive Church, to have public Prayer in the Church, or to minister the Sacraments, in a tongue not understanded of the people (*The Book of Common Prayer*, 872).
2. Much of this is collected in *Stars in a Dark World: Stories of the Saints and Holy Days of the Liturgy* by John Julian, OJN (Parker, CO: Outskirts Press, 2009).
3. Robert P. Smith, *On Pressing the Apostle Paul: Attesting the Pastoral and Prophetic Vision of The Episcopal Church*, 2006.

Looking for Life

1. See www.city-data.com/zips/20662.html; www.pr.dfms.org/study/StaticPDFs/2/2489-0030.pdf; www.pr.dfms.org/study/exports/2489-0030_20110409_07223824.pdf.
2. Josephine H. Hicks, *If There's Anything I Can Do: What You Can Do When Serious Illness Strikes* (Chicago: JHH Publications, 2011).

Living Abundantly

1. Baptismal Covenant, *The Book of Common Prayer* (New York: Church Hymnal Corporation, 1979), 613.

Nourished by the World

1. See http://www.choosemyplate.gov/

Jesus: Our GPS

1. See www.newyork.cbslocal.com/2011/06/21/housekeeper-sues-indian-diplomat-prabhu-dayal-in-nyc-over-wages/.

Nurturing New Believers

1. Glyn Williams, *Captain Cook: Explorer, Navigator and Pioneer*. BBC. www.bbc.co.uk/history/british/empire_seapower/captaincook_01.shtml.

The Freedom to Serve

1. Hisonori Kano, *Nikkei Farmer on the Nebraska Plains: A Memoir* (Lubbock, TX: Texas Tech University Press, 2010).

Healing and Wholeness

1. See www.bloomberg.com/news/2010-11-07/india-s-deadly-diabetes-scourge-cuts-down-millions-rising-to-middle-class.html.
2. See www.unaids.org/en/media/unaids/contentassets/documents/unaidspublication/2011/JC2216_WorldAIDSday_report_2011_en.pdf.
3. All the statistics in this section are from the UN MDG Report for 2011: http://mdgs.un.org/unsd/mdg/Resources/Static/Products/Progress2011/11-31339%20(E)%20MDG%20Report%202011_Book%20LR.pdf.

The Quest for Justice

1. Recall that "economy" has a root meaning of "the house rules" (*oikos* + *nomos*).

Turning the Tables

1. Cheyne-Stokes syndrome involves alternating between conscious deep breathing and apnea. While it strikes healthy people at altitude, it's also characteristic of some who are actively dying.

Minding the Gap

1. John Gillespie Magee Jr., "High Flight (An Airman's Ecstasy)," 1941.

Created for Life

1. Like what Desmond Tutu said about Jesus's command to feed people: "He didn't tell us to stand around and wait for pizzas to fall from heaven!"

Casting Out Demons

1. See www.dfms.org/80050_125046_ENG_HTM.htm.

Traveling Light

1. S. C. Gwynne, *Empire of the Summer Moon: Quanah Parker and the Rise and Fall of the Comanches, the Most Powerful Indian Tribe in American History* (New York: Scribner, 2010).

Sharing the Wealth

1. See www.churchworldservice.org/PDFs/Resources/Hunger.pdf.
2. See www.feedingamerica.org/hunger-in-america/hunger-facts/hunger-and-poverty-statistics.aspx.
3. See the *New York Times* website, www.nytimes.com/2011/07/01/us/01orlando.html?scp=1&sq=+Orlando+food+not+bombs&st=nyt.

4. See www.usgovernmentspending.com/budget_gs.php?span=
   usgs302&year=2011&view=1&expand=406080837041&expandC=
   &units=b&fy=fy12&local=undefined&state=US#usgs30240.
5. See www.slate.com/id/2266025/entry/2266026/.

Living in Joyful Hope
1. See www.episcopalservicecorps.org/program2.php?id=11.

Transforming the Planet
1. Nelle Morton, *The Journey Is Home* (Boston: Beacon, 1985).

Suggestions for Further Reading

Alkire, Sabina and Edmund Newell. *What Can One Person Do? Faith to Heal a Broken World*. New York: Church Publishing, 2005.

Brainard, Lael and Derek Chollet, eds. *Global Development 2.0: Can Philanthropists, the Public, and the Poor Make Poverty History?* Washington, DC: Brookings Institution, 2008.

Collier, Paul. *The Bottom Billion: Why the Poorest Countries Are Failing and What Can Be Done About It*. New York: Oxford University Press, 2007.

Daley-Harris, Shannon and Jeffrey Keenan. *Our Day to End Poverty: 24 Ways You Can Make a Difference*. San Francisco: Berrett-Koehler, 2007.

Jones, Van. *The Green Collar Economy: How One Solution Can Fix Our Two Biggest Problems*. New York: HarperOne, 2008.

Lyman, Princeton and Patricia Dorff, eds. *Beyond Humanitarianism: What You Need to Know about Africa and Why It Matters*. New York: Council on Foreign Relations, 2007.

McGovern, George, Bob Dole and Donald E. Messer. *Ending Hunger Now: A Challenge to Persons of Faith*. Minneapolis: Augsburg Fortress, 2005.

Moore, Kathleen Dean and Michael Nelson, eds. *Moral Ground: Ethical Action for a Planet in Peril*. San Antonio: Trinity, 2011.

Payne, Ruby K. *A Framework for Understanding Poverty*. 4th ed. Highlands, TX: Aha! Process, 1996.

Sachs, Jeffrey. *Common Wealth: Economics for a Crowded Planet*. New York: Penguin, 2008.
———. *The End of Poverty: Economic Possibilities for Our Time*. New York: Penguin, 2005.

Sacks, Jonathan. *The Home We Build Together: Recreating Society*. New York: Continuum, 2007.

Schori, Katharine Jefferts. *The Heartbeat of God: Finding the Sacred in the Middle of Everything*. Woodstock, VT: SkyLight Paths, 2010.

Tanner, Kathryn. *Economy of Grace*. Minneapolis: Augsburg Fortress, 2005.

Inspiration

Restoring Life's Missing Pieces
The Spiritual Power of Remembering & Reuniting with People, Places, Things & Self
by Caren Goldman
A powerful and thought-provoking look at reunions of all kinds as roads to remembering and re-membering ourselves.
6 x 9, 208 pp, Quality PB, 978-1-59473-295-9 **$16.99**

How Did I Get to Be 70 When I'm 35 Inside?
Spiritual Surprises of Later Life
by Linda Douty
Encourages you to focus on the inner changes of aging to help you greet your later years as the grand adventure they can be.
6 x 9, 208 pp, Quality PB, 978-1-59473-297-3 **$16.99**

Spiritually Healthy Divorce: Navigating Disruption with Insight & Hope
by Carolyne Call
A spiritual map to help you move through the twists and turns of divorce.
6 x 9, 224 pp, Quality PB, 978-1-59473-288-1 **$16.99**

Who Is My God? 2nd Edition
An Innovative Guide to Finding Your Spiritual Identity
by the Editors at SkyLight Paths
Provides the Spiritual Identity Self-Test™ to uncover the components of your unique spirituality.
6 x 9, 160 pp, Quality PB, 978-1-59473-014-6 **$15.99**

God the *What?*
What Our Metaphors for God Reveal about Our Beliefs in God
by Carolyn Jane Bohler
Inspires you to consider a wide range of images of God in order to refine how you imagine God.
6 x 9, 192 pp, Quality PB, 978-1-59473-251-5 **$16.99**

Journeys of Simplicity
Traveling Light with Thomas Merton, Bashō,
Edward Abbey, Annie Dillard & Others
by Philip Harnden
Invites you to consider a more graceful way of traveling through life.
PB includes journal pages to help you get started on
your own spiritual journey.
5 x 7¼, 144 pp, Quality PB, 978-1-59473-181-5 **$12.99**
5 x 7¼, 128 pp, HC, 978-1-893361-76-8 **$16.95**

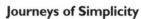

Or phone, fax, mail or e-mail to: SKYLIGHT PATHS Publishing
Sunset Farm Offices, Route 4 • P.O. Box 237 • Woodstock, Vermont 05091
Tel: (802) 457-4000 • Fax: (802) 457-4004 • www.skylightpaths.com
Credit card orders: (800) 962-4544 (8:30AM–5:30PM EST Monday–Friday)
Generous discounts on quantity orders. SATISFACTION GUARANTEED. Prices subject to change.

Judaism / Christianity / Islam / Interfaith

Christians & Jews—Faith to Faith: Tragic History, Promising Present, Fragile Future *by Rabbi James Rudin*
A probing examination of Christian-Jewish relations that looks at the major issues facing both faith communities. 6 x 9, 288 pp, HC, 978-1-58023-432-0 **$24.99***

Getting to the Heart of Interfaith
The Eye-Opening, Hope-Filled Friendship of a Pastor, a Rabbi & an Imam
by Pastor Don Mackenzie, Rabbi Ted Falcon and Imam Jamal Rahman
Offers many insights and encouragements for individuals and groups who want to tap into the promise of interfaith dialogue. 6 x 9, 192 pp, Quality PB, 978-1-59473-263-8 **$16.99**

Hearing the Call across Traditions: Readings on Faith and Service
Edited by Adam Davis; Foreword by Eboo Patel
Explores the connections between faith, service and social justice through the prose, verse and sacred texts of the world's great faith traditions.
6 x 9, 352 pp, Quality PB, 978-1-59473-303-1 **$18.99**; HC, 978-1-59473-264-5 **$29.99**

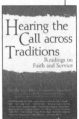

How to Do Good & Avoid Evil: A Global Ethic from the Sources of Judaism
by Hans Küng and Rabbi Walter Homolka; Translated by Rev. Dr. John Bowden
6 x 9, 224 pp, HC, 978-1-59473-255-3 **$19.99**

Blessed Relief: What Christians Can Learn from Buddhists about Suffering
by Gordon Peerman 6 x 9, 208 pp, Quality PB, 978-1-59473-252-2 **$16.99**

The Changing Christian World: A Brief Introduction for Jews
by Rabbi Leonard A. Schoolman 5½ x 8½, 176 pp, Quality PB, 978-1-58023-344-6 **$16.99***

Christians & Jews in Dialogue: Learning in the Presence of the Other *by Mary C. Boys and Sara S. Lee; Foreword by Dorothy C. Bass* 6 x 9, 240 pp, Quality PB, 978-1-59473-254-6 **$18.99**

Disaster Spiritual Care: Practical Clergy Responses to Community, Regional and National Tragedy *Edited by Rabbi Stephen B. Roberts, BCJC, and Rev. Willard W.C. Ashley, Sr., DMin, DH*
6 x 9, 384 pp, HC, 978-1-59473-240-9 **$50.00**

InterActive Faith: The Essential Interreligious Community-Building Handbook
Edited by Rev. Bud Heckman with Rori Picker Neiss; Foreword by Rev. Dirk Ficca
6 x 9, 304 pp, Quality PB, 978-1-59473-273-7 **$16.99**; HC, 978-1-59473-237-9 **$29.99**

The Jewish Approach to God: A Brief Introduction for Christians
by Rabbi Neil Gillman, PhD 5½ x 8½, 192 pp, Quality PB, 978-1-58023-190-9 **$16.95***

The Jewish Approach to Repairing the World (Tikkun Olam): A Brief Introduction for Christians *by Rabbi Elliot N. Dorff, PhD, with Rev. Cory Willson*
5½ x 8½, 256 pp, Quality PB, 978-1-58023-349-1 **$16.99***

The Jewish Connection to Israel, the Promised Land: A Brief Introduction for Christians *by Rabbi Eugene Korn, PhD* 5½ x 8½, 192 pp, Quality PB, 978-1-58023-318-7 **$14.99***

Jewish Holidays: A Brief Introduction for Christians *by Rabbi Kerry M. Olitzky and Rabbi Daniel Judson* 5½ x 8½, 176 pp, Quality PB, 978-1-58023-302-6 **$16.99***

Jewish Ritual: A Brief Introduction for Christians
by Rabbi Kerry M. Olitzky and Rabbi Daniel Judson 5½ x 8½, 144 pp, Quality PB, 978-1-58023-210-4 **$14.99***

Jewish Spirituality: A Brief Introduction for Christians *by Rabbi Lawrence Kushner*
5½ x 8½, 112 pp, Quality PB, 978-1-58023-150-3 **$12.95***

A Jewish Understanding of the New Testament *by Rabbi Samuel Sandmel;*
New preface by Rabbi David Sandmel 5½ x 8½, 368 pp, Quality PB, 978-1-59473-048-1 **$19.99***

Modern Jews Engage the New Testament: Enhancing Jewish Well-Being in a Christian Environment *by Rabbi Michael J. Cook, PhD* 6 x 9, 416 pp, HC, 978-1-58023-313-2 **$29.99***

Talking about God: Exploring the Meaning of Religious Life with Kierkegaard, Buber, Tillich and Heschel *by Daniel F. Polish, PhD* 6 x 9, 160 pp, Quality PB, 978-1-59473-272-0 **$16.99**

We Jews and Jesus: Exploring Theological Differences for Mutual Understanding
by Rabbi Samuel Sandmel; New preface by Rabbi David Sandmel
6 x 9, 192 pp, Quality PB, 978-1-59473-208-9 **$16.99**

Who Are the *Real* Chosen People? The Meaning of Chosenness in Judaism, Christianity and Islam *by Reuven Firestone, PhD*
6 x 9, 176 pp, Quality PB, 978-1-59473-290-4 **$16.99**; HC, 978-1-59473-248-5 **$21.99**

* A book from Jewish Lights, SkyLight Paths' sister imprint

Sacred Texts—SkyLight Illuminations Series

Offers today's spiritual seeker an enjoyable entry into the great classic texts of the world's spiritual traditions. Each classic is presented in an accessible translation, with facing pages of guided commentary from experts, giving you the keys you need to understand the history, context and meaning of the text.

CHRISTIANITY

Celtic Christian Spirituality: Essential Writings—Annotated & Explained
Annotation by Mary C. Earle; Foreword by John Philip Newell
Explores how the writings of this lively tradition embody the gospel.
5½ x 8½, 176 pp, Quality PB, 978-1-59473-302-4 **$16.99**

The End of Days: Essential Selections from Apocalyptic Texts—
Annotated & Explained *Annotation by Robert G. Clouse, PhD*
Helps you understand the complex Christian visions of the end of the world.
5½ x 8½, 224 pp, Quality PB, 978-1-59473-170-9 **$16.99**

The Hidden Gospel of Matthew: Annotated & Explained
Translation & Annotation by Ron Miller Discover the words and events that have the strongest connection to the historical Jesus.
5½ x 8½, 272 pp, Quality PB, 978-1-59473-038-2 **$16.99**

The Infancy Gospels of Jesus: Apocryphal Tales from the Childhoods of Mary and Jesus—Annotated & Explained
Translation & Annotation by Stevan Davies; Foreword by A. Edward Siecienski, PhD
A startling presentation of the early lives of Mary, Jesus and other biblical figures that will amuse and surprise you. 5½ x 8½, 176 pp, Quality PB, 978-1-59473-258-4 **$16.99**

The Lost Sayings of Jesus: Teachings from Ancient Christian, Jewish, Gnostic and Islamic Sources—Annotated & Explained
Translation & Annotation by Andrew Phillip Smith; Foreword by Stephan A. Hoeller
This collection of more than three hundred sayings depicts Jesus as a Wisdom teacher who speaks to people of all faiths as a mystic and spiritual master.
5½ x 8½, 240 pp, Quality PB, 978-1-59473-172-3 **$16.99**

Philokalia: The Eastern Christian Spiritual Texts—Selections
Annotated & Explained *Annotation by Allyne Smith; Translation by G. E. H. Palmer, Phillip Sherrard and Bishop Kallistos Ware*
The first approachable introduction to the wisdom of the Philokalia, the classic text of Eastern Christian spirituality. 5¼ x 8¼, 240 pp, Quality PB, 978-1-59473-103-7 **$16.99**

The Sacred Writings of Paul: Selections Annotated & Explained
Translation & Annotation by Ron Miller Leads you into the exciting immediacy of Paul's teachings. 5½ x 8½, 224 pp, Quality PB, 978-1-59473-213-3 **$16.99**

Saint Augustine of Hippo: Selections from *Confessions* and Other Essential Writings—Annotated & Explained
Annotation by Joseph T. Kelley, PhD; Translation by the Augustinian Heritage Institute
Provides insight into the mind and heart of this foundational Christian figure.
5½ x 8½, 272 pp, Quality PB, 978-1-59473-282-9 **$16.99**

St. Ignatius Loyola—The Spiritual Writings: Selections Annotated & Explained *Annotation by Mark Mossa, SJ*
Draws from contemporary translations of original texts focusing on the practical mysticism of Ignatius of Loyola. 5½ x 8½, 224 pp (est), Quality PB, 978-1-59473-301-7 **$16.99**

Sex Texts from the Bible: Selections Annotated & Explained
Translation & Annotation by Teresa J. Hornsby; Foreword by Amy-Jill Levine
Demystifies the Bible's ideas on gender roles, marriage, sexual orientation, virginity, lust and sexual pleasure. 5½ x 8½, 208 pp, Quality PB, 978-1-59473-217-1 **$16.99**

Sacred Texts—continued

CHRISTIANITY—continued

Spiritual Writings on Mary: Annotated & Explained
Annotation by Mary Ford-Grabowsky; Foreword by Andrew Harvey
Examines the role of Mary, the mother of Jesus, as a source of inspiration in history and in life today. 5½ x 8½, 288 pp, Quality PB, 978-1-59473-001-6 **$16.99**

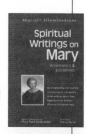

The Way of a Pilgrim: The Jesus Prayer Journey—Annotated & Explained
Translation & Annotation by Gleb Pokrovsky; Foreword by Andrew Harvey
A classic of Russian Orthodox spirituality.
5½ x 8½, 160 pp, Illus., Quality PB, 978-1-893361-31-7 **$14.95**

GNOSTICISM

Gnostic Writings on the Soul: Annotated & Explained
Translation & Annotation by Andrew Phillip Smith; Foreword by Stephan A. Hoeller
Reveals the inspiring ways your soul can remember and return to its unique, divine purpose. 5½ x 8½, 144 pp, Quality PB, 978-1-59473-220-1 **$16.99**

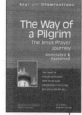

The Gospel of Philip: Annotated & Explained
Translation & Annotation by Andrew Phillip Smith; Foreword by Stevan Davies
Reveals otherwise unrecorded sayings of Jesus and fragments of Gnostic mythology.
5½ x 8½, 160 pp, Quality PB, 978-1-59473-111-2 **$16.99**

The Gospel of Thomas: Annotated & Explained
Translation & Annotation by Stevan Davies; Foreword by Andrew Harvey
Sheds new light on the origins of Christianity and portrays Jesus as a wisdom-loving sage.
5½ x 8½, 192 pp, Quality PB, 978-1-893361-45-4 **$16.99**

The Secret Book of John: The Gnostic Gospel—Annotated & Explained
Translation & Annotation by Stevan Davies The most significant and influential text of the ancient Gnostic religion. 5½ x 8½, 208 pp, Quality PB, 978-1-59473-082-5 **$16.99**

JUDAISM

The Divine Feminine in Biblical Wisdom Literature
Selections Annotated & Explained
Translation & Annotation by Rabbi Rami Shapiro; Foreword by Rev. Cynthia Bourgeault, PhD
Uses the Hebrew Bible and Wisdom literature to explain Sophia's way of wisdom and illustrate Her creative energy. 5½ x 8½, 240 pp, Quality PB, 978-1-59473-109-9 **$16.99**

Ecclesiastes: Annotated & Explained
Translation & Annotation by Rabbi Rami Shapiro; Foreword by Rev. Barbara Cawthorne Crafton
A timeless teaching on living well amid uncertainty and insecurity.
5½ x 8½, 160 pp, Quality PB, 978-1-59473-287-4 **$16.99**

Ethics of the Sages: *Pirke Avot*—Annotated & Explained
Translation & Annotation by Rabbi Rami Shapiro Clarifies the ethical teachings of the early Rabbis. 5½ x 8½, 192 pp, Quality PB, 978-1-59473-207-2 **$16.99**

Hasidic Tales: Annotated & Explained
Translation & Annotation by Rabbi Rami Shapiro; Foreword by Andrew Harvey
Introduces the legendary tales of the impassioned Hasidic rabbis, presenting them as stories rather than as parables. 5½ x 8½, 240 pp, Quality PB, 978-1-893361-86-7 **$16.95**

The Hebrew Prophets: Selections Annotated & Explained
Translation & Annotation by Rabbi Rami Shapiro; Foreword by Rabbi Zalman M. Schachter-Shalomi
5½ x 8½, 224 pp, Quality PB, 978-1-59473-037-5 **$16.99**

Tanya, the Masterpiece of Hasidic Wisdom: Selections Annotated & Explained *Translation & Annotation by Rabbi Rami Shapiro; Foreword by Rabbi Zalman M. Schachter-Shalomi* Clarifies one of the most powerful and potentially transformative books of Jewish wisdom. 5½ x 8½, 240 pp, Quality PB, 978-1-59473-275-1 **$16.99**

Zohar: Annotated & Explained *Translation & Annotation by Daniel C. Matt; Foreword by Andrew Harvey* The canonical text of Jewish mystical tradition.
5½ x 8½, 176 pp, Quality PB, 978-1-893361-51-5 **$15.99**

Bible Stories / Folktales

Abraham's Bind & Other Bible Tales of Trickery, Folly, Mercy and Love by Michael J. Caduto
New retellings of episodes in the lives of familiar biblical characters explore relevant life lessons. 6 x 9, 224 pp, HC, 978-1-59473-186-0 **$19.99**

Daughters of the Desert: Stories of Remarkable Women from Christian, Jewish and Muslim Traditions by Claire Rudolf Murphy,
Meghan Nuttall Sayres, Mary Cronk Farrell, Sarah Conover and Betsy Wharton
Breathes new life into the old tales of our female ancestors in faith. Uses traditional scriptural passages as starting points, then with vivid detail fills in historical context and place. Chapters reveal the voices of Sarah, Hagar, Huldah, Esther, Salome, Mary Magdalene, Lydia, Khadija, Fatima and many more. Historical fiction ideal for readers of all ages.
5½ x 8½, 192 pp, Quality PB, 978-1-59473-106-8 **$14.99** Inc. reader's discussion guide
HC, 978-1-893361-72-0 **$19.95**

The Triumph of Eve & Other Subversive Bible Tales
by Matt Biers-Ariel
These engaging retellings of familiar Bible stories are witty, often hilarious and always profound. They invite you to grapple with questions and issues that are often hidden in the original texts.
5½ x 8½, 192 pp, Quality PB, 978-1-59473-176-1 **$14.99**
Also available: **The Triumph of Eve Teacher's Guide**
8½ x 11, 44 pp, PB, 978-1-59473-152-5 **$8.99**

Wisdom in the Telling
Finding Inspiration and Grace in Traditional Folktales and Myths Retold
by Lorraine Hartin-Gelardi
6 x 9, 192 pp, HC, 978-1-59473-185-3 **$19.99**

Religious Etiquette / Reference

How to Be a Perfect Stranger, 5th Edition: The Essential Religious Etiquette Handbook Edited by Stuart M. Matlins and Arthur J. Magida
The indispensable guidebook to help the well-meaning guest when visiting other people's religious ceremonies. A straightforward guide to the rituals and celebrations of the major religions and denominations in the United States and Canada from the perspective of an interested guest of any other faith, based on information obtained from authorities of each religion. Belongs in every living room, library and office. Covers:
African American Methodist Churches • Assemblies of God • Bahá'í Faith • Baptist • Buddhist • Christian Church (Disciples of Christ) • Christian Science (Church of Christ, Scientist) • Churches of Christ • Episcopalian and Anglican • Hindu • Islam • Jehovah's Witnesses • Jewish • Lutheran • Mennonite/Amish • Methodist • Mormon (Church of Jesus Christ of Latter-day Saints) • Native American/First Nations • Orthodox Churches • Pentecostal Church of God • Presbyterian • Quaker (Religious Society of Friends) • Reformed Church in America/Canada • Roman Catholic • Seventh-day Adventist • Sikh • Unitarian Universalist • United Church of Canada • United Church of Christ

"The things Miss Manners forgot to tell us about religion."

—*Los Angeles Times*

"Finally, for those inclined to undertake their own spiritual journeys ... tells visitors what to expect."   —*New York Times*

6 x 9, 432 pp, Quality PB, 978-1-59473-294-2 **$19.99**

The Perfect Stranger's Guide to Funerals and Grieving Practices: A Guide
to Etiquette in Other People's Religious Ceremonies Edited by Stuart M. Matlins
6 x 9, 240 pp, Quality PB, 978-1-893361-20-1 **$16.95**

The Perfect Stranger's Guide to Wedding Ceremonies: A Guide to
Etiquette in Other People's Religious Ceremonies Edited by Stuart M. Matlins
6 x 9, 208 pp, Quality PB, 978-1-893361-19-5 **$16.95**

Spirituality

The Heartbeat of God: Finding the Sacred in the Middle of Everything
by Katharine Jefferts Schori; Foreword by Joan Chittister, OSB
Explores our connections to other people, to other nations and with the environment through the lens of faith. 6 x 9, 240 pp, HC, 978-1-59473-292-8 **$21.99**

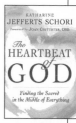

A Dangerous Dozen: Twelve Christians Who Threatened the Status Quo but Taught Us to Live Like Jesus
by the Rev. Canon C. K. Robertson, PhD; Foreword by Archbishop Desmond Tutu
Profiles twelve visionary men and women who challenged society and showed the world a different way of living. 6 x 9, 208 pp, Quality PB, 978-1-59473-298-0 **$16.99**

Decision Making & Spiritual Discernment: The Sacred Art of Finding Your Way *by Nancy L. Bieber*
Presents three essential aspects of Spirit-led decision making: willingness, attentiveness and responsiveness. 5½ x 8½, 208 pp, Quality PB, 978-1-59473-289-8 **$16.99**

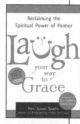

Laugh Your Way to Grace: Reclaiming the Spiritual Power of Humor
by Rev. Susan Sparks A powerful, humorous case for laughter as a spiritual, healing path. 6 x 9, 176 pp, Quality PB, 978-1-59473-280-5 **$16.99**

Living into Hope: A Call to Spiritual Action for Such a Time as This
by Rev. Dr. Joan Brown Campbell; Foreword by Karen Armstrong
A visionary minister speaks out on the pressing issues that face us today, offering inspiration and challenge. 6 x 9, 208 pp, HC, 978-1-59473-283-6 **$21.99**

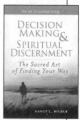

Claiming Earth as Common Ground: The Ecological Crisis through the Lens of Faith
by Andrea Cohen-Kiener; Foreword by Rev. Sally Bingham
6 x 9, 192 pp, Quality PB, 978-1-59473-261-4 **$16.99**

Bread, Body, Spirit: Finding the Sacred in Food
Edited and with Introductions by Alice Peck 6 x 9, 224 pp, Quality PB, 978-1-59473-242-3 **$19.99**

Creating a Spiritual Retirement: A Guide to the Unseen Possibilities in Our Lives
by Molly Srode 6 x 9, 208 pp, b/w photos, Quality PB, 978-1-59473-050-4 **$14.99**

Creative Aging: Rethinking Retirement and Non-Retirement in a Changing World
by Marjory Zoet Bankson 6 x 9, 160 pp, Quality PB, 978-1-59473-281-2 **$16.99**

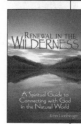

Keeping Spiritual Balance as We Grow Older: More than 65 Creative Ways to Use Purpose, Prayer, and the Power of Spirit to Build a Meaningful Retirement
by Molly and Bernie Srode 8 x 8, 224 pp, Quality PB, 978-1-59473-042-9 **$16.99**

Hearing the Call across Traditions: Readings on Faith and Service
Edited by Adam Davis; Foreword by Eboo Patel
6 x 9, 352 pp, Quality PB, 978-1-59473-303-1 **$18.99**; HC, 978-1-59473-264-5 **$29.99**

Honoring Motherhood: Prayers, Ceremonies & Blessings
Edited and with Introductions by Lynn L. Caruso 5 x 7¼, 272 pp, HC, 978-1-59473-239-3 **$19.99**

Journeys of Simplicity: Traveling Light with Thomas Merton, Bashō, Edward Abbey, Annie Dillard & Others *by Philip Harnden*
5 x 7¼, 144 pp, Quality PB, 978-1-59473-181-5 **$12.99**; 128 pp, HC, 978-1-893361-76-8 **$16.95**

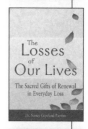

The Losses of Our Lives: The Sacred Gifts of Renewal in Everyday Loss
by Dr. Nancy Copeland-Payton 6 x 9, 192 pp, HC, 978-1-59473-271-3 **$19.99**

Renewal in the Wilderness: A Spiritual Guide to Connecting with God in the Natural World *by John Lionberger*
6 x 9, 176 pp, b/w photos, Quality PB, 978-1-59473-219-5 **$16.99**

Soul Fire: Accessing Your Creativity
by Thomas Ryan, CSP 6 x 9, 160 pp, Quality PB, 978-1-59473-243-0 **$16.99**

A Spirituality for Brokenness: Discovering Your Deepest Self in Difficult Times
by Terry Taylor 6 x 9, 176 pp, Quality PB, 978-1-59473-229-4 **$16.99**

A Walk with Four Spiritual Guides: Krishna, Buddha, Jesus, and Ramakrishna
by Andrew Harvey 5½ x 8½, 192 pp, b/w photos & illus., Quality PB, 978-1-59473-138-9 **$15.99**

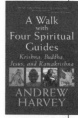

The Workplace and Spirituality: New Perspectives on Research and Practice
Edited by Dr. Joan Marques, Dr. Satinder Dhiman and Dr. Richard King
6 x 9, 256 pp, HC, 978-1-59473-260-7 **$29.99**

Spirituality & Crafts

Beading—The Creative Spirit: Finding Your Sacred Center through the Art of Beadwork *by Rev. Wendy Ellsworth*
Invites you on a spiritual pilgrimage into the kaleidoscope world of glass and color. 7 x 9, 240 pp, 8-page color insert, 40+ b/w photos and 40 diagrams, Quality PB, 978-1-59473-267-6 **$18.99**

Contemplative Crochet: A Hands-On Guide for Interlocking Faith and Craft *by Cindy Crandall-Frazier; Foreword by Linda Skolnik*
Illuminates the spiritual lessons you can learn through crocheting.
7 x 9, 208 pp, b/w photos, Quality PB, 978-1-59473-238-6 **$16.99**

The Knitting Way: A Guide to Spiritual Self-Discovery
by Linda Skolnik and Janice MacDaniels Examines how you can explore and strengthen your spiritual life through knitting.
7 x 9, 240 pp, b/w photos, Quality PB, 978-1-59473-079-5 **$16.99**

The Painting Path: Embodying Spiritual Discovery through Yoga, Brush and Color *by Linda Novick; Foreword by Richard Segalman*
Explores the divine connection you can experience through art.
7 x 9, 208 pp, 8-page color insert, plus b/w photos, Quality PB, 978-1-59473-226-3 **$18.99**

The Quilting Path: A Guide to Spiritual Discovery through Fabric, Thread and Kabbalah *by Louise Silk*
Explores how to cultivate personal growth through quilt making.
7 x 9, 192 pp, b/w photos and illus., Quality PB, 978-1-59473-206-5 **$16.99**

The Scrapbooking Journey: A Hands-On Guide to Spiritual Discovery
by Cory Richardson-Lauve; Foreword by Stacy Julian Reveals how this craft can become a practice used to deepen and shape your life.
7 x 9, 176 pp, 8-page color insert, plus b/w photos, Quality PB, 978-1-59473-216-4 **$18.99**

The Soulwork of Clay: A Hands-On Approach to Spirituality
by Marjory Zoet Bankson; Photos by Peter Bankson
Takes you through the seven-step process of making clay into a pot, drawing parallels at each stage to the process of spiritual growth.
7 x 9, 192 pp, b/w photos, Quality PB, 978-1-59473-249-2 **$16.99**

Kabbalah / Enneagram
(Books from Jewish Lights Publishing, SkyLight Paths' sister imprint)

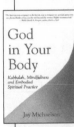

Cast in God's Image: Discover Your Personality Type Using the Enneagram and Kabbalah
by Rabbi Howard A. Addison, PhD 7 x 9, 176 pp, Quality PB, 978-1-58023-124-4 **$16.95**

Ehyeh: A Kabbalah for Tomorrow *by Rabbi Arthur Green, PhD*
6 x 9, 224 pp, Quality PB, 978-1-58023-213-5 **$18.99**

The Enneagram and Kabbalah, 2nd Edition: Reading Your Soul
by Rabbi Howard A. Addison, PhD 6 x 9, 192 pp, Quality PB, 978-1-58023-229-6 **$16.99**

The Gift of Kabbalah: Discovering the Secrets of Heaven, Renewing Your Life on Earth
by Tamar Frankiel, PhD 6 x 9, 256 pp, Quality PB, 978-1-58023-141-1 **$16.95**

God in Your Body: Kabbalah, Mindfulness and Embodied Spiritual Practice
by Jay Michaelson 6 x 9, 272 pp, Quality PB, 978-1-58023-304-0 **$18.99**

Jewish Mysticism and the Spiritual Life: Classical Texts, Contemporary Reflections
Edited by Dr. Lawrence Fine, Dr. Eitan Fishbane and Rabbi Or N. Rose
6 x 9, 256 pp, HC, 978-1-58023-434-4 **$24.99**

Kabbalah: A Brief Introduction for Christians
by Tamar Frankiel, PhD 5½ x 8½, 208 pp, Quality PB, 978-1-58023-303-3 **$16.99**

Zohar: Annotated & Explained *Translation & Annotation by Daniel C. Matt; Foreword by Andrew Harvey* 5½ x 8½, 176 pp, Quality PB, 978-1-893361-51-5 **$15.99**

Spiritual Practice

Fly Fishing—The Sacred Art: Casting a Fly as a Spiritual Practice
by Rabbi Eric Eisenkramer and Rev. Michael Attas, MD
Illuminates what fly fishing can teach you about reflection, awe and wonder; the benefits of solitude; the blessing of community and the search for the Divine.
5½ x 8½, 192 pp (est), Quality PB, 978-1-59473-299-7 **$16.99**

***Lectio Divina*—The Sacred Art:** Transforming Words & Images into Heart-Centered Prayer *by Christine Valters Paintner, PhD*
Expands the practice of sacred reading beyond scriptural texts and makes it accessible in contemporary life. 5½ x 8½, 240 pp, Quality PB, 978-1-59473-300-0 **$16.99**

Haiku—The Sacred Art: A Spiritual Practice in Three Lines
by Margaret D. McGee 5½ x 8½, 192 pp, Quality PB, 978-1-59473-269-0 **$16.99**

Dance—The Sacred Art: The Joy of Movement as a Spiritual Practice
by Cynthia Winton-Henry 5½ x 8½, 224 pp, Quality PB, 978-1-59473-268-3 **$16.99**

Spiritual Adventures in the Snow: Skiing & Snowboarding as Renewal for Your Soul
by Dr. Marcia McFee and Rev. Karen Foster; Foreword by Paul Arthur
5½ x 8½, 208 pp, Quality PB, 978-1-59473-270-6 **$16.99**

Divining the Body: Reclaim the Holiness of Your Physical Self *by Jan Phillips*
8 x 8, 256 pp, Quality PB, 978-1-59473-080-1 **$16.99**

Everyday Herbs in Spiritual Life: A Guide to Many Practices
by Michael J. Caduto; Foreword by Rosemary Gladstar
7 x 9, 208 pp, 20+ b/w illus., Quality PB, 978-1-59473-174-7 **$16.99**

Giving—The Sacred Art: Creating a Lifestyle of Generosity
by Lauren Tyler Wright 5½ x 8½, 208 pp, Quality PB, 978-1-59473-224-9 **$16.99**

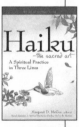

Hospitality—The Sacred Art: Discovering the Hidden Spiritual Power of Invitation and Welcome *by Rev. Nanette Sawyer; Foreword by Rev. Dirk Ficca*
5½ x 8½, 208 pp, Quality PB, 978-1-59473-228-7 **$16.99**

Labyrinths from the Outside In: Walking to Spiritual Insight—A Beginner's Guide
by Donna Schaper and Carole Ann Camp
6 x 9, 208 pp, b/w illus. and photos, Quality PB, 978-1-893361-18-8 **$16.95**

Practicing the Sacred Art of Listening: A Guide to Enrich Your Relationships and Kindle Your Spiritual Life *by Kay Lindahl* 8 x 8, 176 pp, Quality PB, 978-1-893361-85-0 **$16.95**

Recovery—The Sacred Art: The Twelve Steps as Spiritual Practice *by Rami Shapiro; Foreword by Joan Borysenko, PhD* 5½ x 8½, 240 pp, Quality PB, 978-1-59473-259-1 **$16.99**

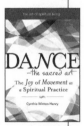

Running—The Sacred Art: Preparing to Practice *by Dr. Warren A. Kay; Foreword by Kristin Armstrong* 5½ x 8½, 160 pp, Quality PB, 978-1-59473-227-0 **$16.99**

The Sacred Art of Chant: Preparing to Practice
by Ana Hernández 5½ x 8½, 192 pp, Quality PB, 978-1-59473-036-8 **$15.99**

The Sacred Art of Fasting: Preparing to Practice
by Thomas Ryan, CSP 5½ x 8½, 192 pp, Quality PB, 978-1-59473-078-8 **$15.99**

The Sacred Art of Forgiveness: Forgiving Ourselves and Others through God's Grace
by Marcia Ford 8 x 8, 176 pp, Quality PB, 978-1-59473-175-4 **$18.99**

The Sacred Art of Listening: Forty Reflections for Cultivating a Spiritual Practice
by Kay Lindahl; Illus. by Amy Schnapper 8 x 8, 160 pp, b/w illus., Quality PB, 978-1-893361-44-7 **$16.99**

The Sacred Art of Lovingkindness: Preparing to Practice
by Rabbi Rami Shapiro; Foreword by Marcia Ford 5½ x 8½, 176 pp, Quality PB, 978-1-59473-151-8 **$16.99**

Sacred Attention: A Spiritual Practice for Finding God in the Moment
by Margaret D. McGee 6 x 9, 144 pp, Quality PB, 978-1-59473-291-1 **$16.99**

Soul Fire: Accessing Your Creativity
by Thomas Ryan, CSP 6 x 9, 160 pp, Quality PB, 978-1-59473-243-0 **$16.99**

Thanking & Blessing—The Sacred Art: Spiritual Vitality through Gratefulness
by Jay Marshall, PhD; Foreword by Philip Gulley 5½ x 8½, 176 pp, Quality PB, 978-1-59473-231-7 **$16.99**

Women's Interest

Women, Spirituality and Transformative Leadership
Where Grace Meets Power
Edited by Kathe Schaaf, Kay Lindahl, Kathleen S. Hurty, PhD, and Reverend Guo Cheen
A dynamic conversation on the power of women's spiritual leadership and its emerging patterns of transformation.
6 x 9, 288 pp, Hardcover, 978-1-59473-313-0 **$24.99**

Spiritually Healthy Divorce: Navigating Disruption with Insight & Hope
by Carolyne Call A spiritual map to help you move through the twists and turns of divorce.   6 x 9, 224 pp, Quality PB, 978-1-59473-288-1 **$16.99**

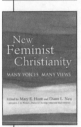

New Feminist Christianity: Many Voices, Many Views
Edited by Mary E. Hunt and Diann L. Neu
Insights from ministers and theologians, activists and leaders, artists and liturgists who are shaping the future. Taken together, their voices offer a starting point for building new models of religious life and worship.
6 x 9, 384 pp, HC, 978-1-59473-285-0 **$24.99**

New Jewish Feminism: Probing the Past, Forging the Future
Edited by Rabbi Elyse Goldstein; Foreword by Anita Diamant
Looks at the growth and accomplishments of Jewish feminism and what they mean for Jewish women today and tomorrow. Features the voices of women from every area of Jewish life, addressing the important issues that concern Jewish women.
6 x 9, 480 pp, Quality PB, 978-1-58023-448-1 **$19.99**; HC, 978-1-58023-359-0 **$24.99***

Bread, Body, Spirit: Finding the Sacred in Food
Edited and with Introductions by Alice Peck   6 x 9, 224 pp, Quality PB, 978-1-59473-242-3 **$19.99**

Dance—The Sacred Art: The Joy of Movement as a Spiritual Practice
by Cynthia Winton-Henry 5½ x 8½, 224 pp, Quality PB, 978-1-59473-268-3 **$16.99**

Daughters of the Desert: Stories of Remarkable Women from Christian, Jewish and Muslim Traditions
by Claire Rudolf Murphy, Meghan Nuttall Sayres, Mary Cronk Farrell, Sarah Conover and Betsy Wharton
5½ x 8½, 192 pp, Illus., Quality PB, 978-1-59473-106-8 **$14.99** Inc. reader's discussion guide

The Divine Feminine in Biblical Wisdom Literature
Selections Annotated & Explained
Translation & Annotation by Rabbi Rami Shapiro; Foreword by Rev. Cynthia Bourgeault, PhD
5½ x 8½, 240 pp, Quality PB, 978-1-59473-109-9 **$16.99**

Divining the Body: Reclaim the Holiness of Your Physical Self
by Jan Phillips 8 x 8, 256 pp, Quality PB, 978-1-59473-080-1 **$16.99**

Honoring Motherhood: Prayers, Ceremonies & Blessings
Edited and with Introductions by Lynn L. Caruso 5 x 7¼, 272 pp, HC, 978-1-59473-239-3 **$19.99**

Next to Godliness: Finding the Sacred in Housekeeping
Edited by Alice Peck 6 x 9, 224 pp, Quality PB, 978-1-59473-214-0 **$19.99**

ReVisions: Seeing Torah through a Feminist Lens
by Rabbi Elyse Goldstein 5½ x 8½, 224 pp, Quality PB, 978-1-58023-117-6 **$16.95***

The Triumph of Eve & Other Subversive Bible Tales
by Matt Biers-Ariel 5½ x 8½, 192 pp, Quality PB, 978-1-59473-176-1 **$14.99**

White Fire: A Portrait of Women Spiritual Leaders in America
by Malka Drucker; Photos by Gay Block 7 x 10, 320 pp, b/w photos, HC, 978-1-893361-64-5 **$24.95**

Woman Spirit Awakening in Nature: Growing Into the Fullness of Who You Are
by Nancy Barrett Chickerneo, PhD; Foreword by Eileen Fisher
8 x 8, 224 pp, b/w illus., Quality PB, 978-1-59473-250-8 **$16.99**

Women of Color Pray: Voices of Strength, Faith, Healing, Hope and Courage
Edited and with Introductions by Christal M. Jackson
5 x 7¼, 208 pp, Quality PB, 978-1-59473-077-1 **$15.99**

The Women's Torah Commentary: New Insights from Women Rabbis on the 54 Weekly Torah Portions *Edited by Rabbi Elyse Goldstein*
6 x 9, 496 pp, Quality PB, 978-1-58023-370-5 **$19.99**; HC, 978-1-58023-076-6 **$34.95***

* A book from Jewish Lights, SkyLight Paths' sister imprint

Prayer / Meditation

Sacred Attention: A Spiritual Practice for Finding God in the Moment
by Margaret D. McGee
Framed on the Christian liturgical year, this inspiring guide explores ways to develop a practice of attention as a means of talking—and listening—to God.
6 x 9, 144 pp, Quality PB, 978-1-59473-291-1 **$16.99**

Women of Color Pray: Voices of Strength, Faith, Healing, Hope and Courage
Edited and with Introductions by Christal M. Jackson
Through these prayers, poetry, lyrics, meditations and affirmations, you will share in the strong and undeniable connection women of color share with God.
5 x 7¼, 208 pp, Quality PB, 978-1-59473-077-1 **$15.99**

Secrets of Prayer: A Multifaith Guide to Creating Personal Prayer in Your Life   *by Nancy Corcoran, CSJ*
This compelling, multifaith guidebook offers you companionship and encouragement on the journey to a healthy prayer life. 6 x 9, 160 pp, Quality PB, 978-1-59473-215-7 **$16.99**

Prayers to an Evolutionary God
by William Cleary; Afterword by Diarmuid O'Murchu
Inspired by the spiritual and scientific teachings of Diarmuid O'Murchu and Teilhard de Chardin, reveals that religion and science can be combined to create an expanding view of the universe—an evolutionary faith.
6 x 9, 208 pp, HC, 978-1-59473-006-1 **$21.99**

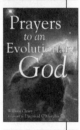

The Art of Public Prayer, 2nd Edition: Not for Clergy Only
by Lawrence A. Hoffman, PhD 6 x 9, 288 pp, Quality PB, 978-1-893361-06-5 **$19.99**

A Heart of Stillness: A Complete Guide to Learning the Art of Meditation
by David A. Cooper 5½ x 8½, 272 pp, Quality PB, 978-1-893361-03-4 **$18.99**

Meditation without Gurus: A Guide to the Heart of Practice
by Clark Strand 5½ x 8½, 192 pp, Quality PB, 978-1-893361-93-5 **$16.95**

Praying with Our Hands: 21 Practices of Embodied Prayer from the World's Spiritual Traditions   *by Jon M. Sweeney; Photos by Jennifer J. Wilson; Foreword by Mother Tessa Bielecki; Afterword by Taitetsu Unno, PhD*
8 x 8, 96 pp, 22 duotone photos, Quality PB, 978-1-893361-16-4 **$16.95**

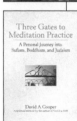

Three Gates to Meditation Practice: A Personal Journey into Sufism, Buddhism, and Judaism   *by David A. Cooper* 5½ x 8½, 240 pp, Quality PB, 978-1-893361-22-5 **$16.95**

Prayer / M. Basil Pennington, OCSO

Finding Grace at the Center, 3rd Edition: The Beginning of Centering Prayer   *with Thomas Keating, OCSO, and Thomas E. Clarke, SJ; Foreword by Rev. Cynthia Bourgeault, PhD* A practical guide to a simple and beautiful form of meditative prayer. 5 x 7¼, 128 pp, Quality PB, 978-1-59473-182-2 **$12.99**

The Monks of Mount Athos: A Western Monk's Extraordinary Spiritual Journey on Eastern Holy Ground   *Foreword by Archimandrite Dionysios*
Explores the landscape, monastic communities and food of Athos.
6 x 9, 352 pp, Quality PB, 978-1-893361-78-2 **$18.95**

Psalms: A Spiritual Commentary   *Illus. by Phillip Ratner*
Reflections on some of the most beloved passages from the Bible's most widely read book.   6 x 9, 176 pp, 24 full-page b/w illus., Quality PB, 978-1-59473-234-8 **$16.99**

The Song of Songs: A Spiritual Commentary   *Illus. by Phillip Ratner*
Explore the Bible's most challenging mystical text.
6 x 9, 160 pp, 14 full-page b/w illus., Quality PB, 978-1-59473-235-5 **$16.99**
HC, 978-1-59473-004-7 **$19.99**

About SKYLIGHT PATHS Publishing

SkyLight Paths Publishing is creating a place where people of different spiritual traditions come together for challenge and inspiration, a place where we can help each other understand the mystery that lies at the heart of our existence.

Through spirituality, our religious beliefs are increasingly becoming a part of our lives—rather than *apart* from our lives. While many of us may be more interested than ever in spiritual growth, we may be less firmly planted in traditional religion. Yet, we do want to deepen our relationship to the sacred, to learn from our own as well as from other faith traditions, and to practice in new ways.

SkyLight Paths sees both believers and seekers as a community that increasingly transcends traditional boundaries of religion and denomination—people wanting to learn from each other, *walking together, finding the way.*

For your information and convenience, at the back of this book we have provided a list of other SkyLight Paths books you might find interesting and useful. They cover the following subjects:

Buddhism / Zen	Global Spiritual	Monasticism
Catholicism	Perspectives	Mysticism
Children's Books	Gnosticism	Poetry
Christianity	Hinduism /	Prayer
Comparative	Vedanta	Religious Etiquette
Religion	Inspiration	Retirement
Current Events	Islam / Sufism	Spiritual Biography
Earth-Based	Judaism	Spiritual Direction
Spirituality	Kabbalah	Spirituality
Enneagram	Meditation	Women's Interest
	Midrash Fiction	Worship

Or phone, fax, mail or e-mail to: SKYLIGHT PATHS Publishing
Sunset Farm Offices, Route 4 • P.O. Box 237 • Woodstock, Vermont 05091
Tel: (802) 457-4000 • Fax: (802) 457-4004 • www.skylightpaths.com
Credit card orders: (800) 962-4544 (8:30AM–5:30PM EST Monday–Friday)
Generous discounts on quantity orders. SATISFACTION GUARANTEED. Prices subject to change.

For more information about each book,
visit our website at www.skylightpaths.com